Don't  :

"Don't [...] at
all o[...].
It's [...]
where [...]?
Like many phrases u[...] n't
judge" comes from the Bible.

In fact, it's a very good motto
for the story which starts after
this introduction. **It's the
story of Jesus, told by
Luke.** You can discover for
yourself how Jesus first used the
expression on page 16 (Luke 6.37).

Throughout Luke's story, we will
discover how Jesus called people to
turn away from judging others, so
that they could grow to understand
one another instead. Again and
again, we see Jesus welcoming,
forgiving, healing and **really
valuing people for who
they are.** He saw other people
as God sees them.

It comes as a shock to most
people to discover that Jesus'
greatest welcome was offered to the
type of people who are most often
judged by others: prostitutes,
beggars, petty criminals, corrupt
officials, and those who turn their
back on religion.

Time Chart ↓

0AD

Birth of Jesus   *Death & Resurrection of Jesus*

Luke's story is told at a leisurely pace. He takes time, so that we can get to know Jesus and all the other characters in the story really well. He seems to be especially concerned for people's circumstances, and what it meant for them to meet Jesus. You won't find a very religious or "churchy" feel to the story, either. Luke is more concerned to show how Jesus talked with people in the ordinary world.

Luke also conveys a great sense of joy in his story. Look at how the story starts. We find an old man, two women (and women had a very limited role at the time) and some shepherds (who were thought of as very low down in society) full of joy because of what God has done for them. Jesus doesn't just welcome and forgive, he also gives people a future worth looking forward to.

Conversion of Paul   Great Fire of Rome

Who was Luke?

We can't be completely sure who Luke was. He was probably a travelling companion of Paul, another great Christian writer, who lived about the same time. In the first few sentences of the story, Luke suggests that he is not an eye witness to the events in Jesus' life, but **someone who has very carefully checked the historical facts** and become convinced of the truth of it for himself.

His concern for detail suggests that Luke may have been a professional historian (and he might also have been a doctor). He was writing to Theophilus about whom we know very little, but who was probably typical of the type of people for whom Luke was writing: Greek and Roman people, living in cities around the Mediterranean towards the end of the first century AD.

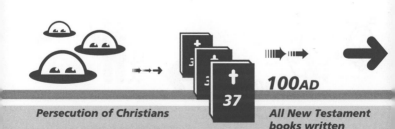

100AD

Persecution of Christians

37

All New Testament books written

The people Luke wrote for came from different religious and social backgrounds, and many of them would have only had a vague idea about the religious ideas and customs of the Jewish people among whom Jesus lived. Some of the people would have been educated in the great classical tradition, and would have warmed to Luke's ordered account. Just as many, however, would have been labourers, fishermen and even slaves, and would have found hope in this story — a story which shows that Jesus affirms the weakest and poorest people in society.

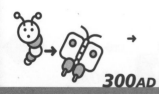

300AD

Conversion of Constantine   **Composition of New Testament agreed**

Why did Luke write?

The fact that we don't know very much about who Luke was, or to whom he was writing, shouldn't worry us too much. What is more important is the focus on Jesus. Luke was in no doubt that Jesus was — and is — of great importance for everyone: he is freely available to all, regardless of status, education, religious background or sex. And Luke wrote his story to support and encourage all those who want to follow Jesus, and who have seen God's truth and glory through him.

Luke was also writing in a relatively new style. He is one of four writers in the Bible who writes about Jesus by telling the story of his life. Twenty or thirty years earlier, Paul had written his famous letters to encourage people in the Christian faith, but he had used the language and ideas of ancient philosophy. Luke's approach was to let people **make up their own minds,** to discover the human face of God, and even to see themselves in the characters and incidents that take place.

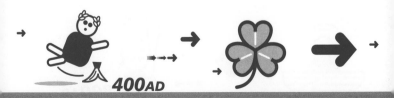

400AD

Fall of Rome **St Patrick in Ireland**

A king and his kingdom

Luke's account of the life and death of Jesus is known as a "Gospel". This is not a religious word, but a military term which described the announcement of a king's victory. It was usual for this to happen when a Roman emperor began his reign, for example. By using the word "Gospel", perhaps early Christians suggested that true authority lies not with the emperor, but with Jesus Christ.

If Jesus is the victorious king, we need to ask what it is like to live in his kingdom.

Luke is quite clear that Jesus' authority comes from the love and forgiveness of God. This may seem crazy but Jesus described life in his kingdom as like being welcomed home after going off the rails (pp.41-2, Luke 15.11-32). God's kingdom is where the most **despised people are loved and accepted** (pp.46-7, Luke 18.9-13) and where the wealthy will have a hard time (p.47, Luke 18.18-27). In short, all our preconceptions about life are turned on their head.

St Augustine in Britain 800AD *Alfred the Great*

Luke saw Jesus as a king, yet he doesn't reign by sitting on a throne, but by being treated as a common criminal and nailed to a cross. If we want to know what God is really like and how much he loves us, Luke points us to the suffering and death of Jesus. The greatest love is the love that shares our hurt and pain, and that is just what Jesus did.

Where does it all end?

The story of Jesus doesn't end with his death on the cross. With the same detail as he tells the rest of the story, Luke ends his gospel with two moving incidents. They tell how Jesus' followers met him after his death, and how they knew for themselves that he was alive (pp.62—4, Luke 24.13—53). The two meetings were each very different, just as people's experience of Jesus was different. What they shared, however, is that sense of joy which is present throughout Luke's story.

1000AD   1200AD

Battle of Hastings   **Magna Carta**

Luke in 30 days

1300AD

John Wycliff translates Bible

Luke's gospel

Why Luke wrote this book

1 Many people have tried to tell the story of what God has done among us. ²They wrote what we had been told by the ones who were there in the beginning and saw what happened. ³So I made a careful study* of everything and then decided to write and tell you exactly what took place. Honourable Theophilus, ⁴I have done this to let you know the truth about what you have heard.

An angel tells about the birth of John

⁵When Herod was king of Judea, there was a priest called Zechariah from the priestly group of Abijah. His wife Elizabeth was from the family of Aaron.* ⁶Both of them were good people and pleased the Lord God by obeying all that he had commanded. ⁷But they did not have children. Elizabeth could not have any, and both Zechariah and Elizabeth were already old.

⁸One day Zechariah's group of priests were on duty, and he was serving God as a priest. ⁹According to the custom of the priests, he had been chosen to go into the Lord's temple that day and to burn incense,* ¹⁰while the people stood outside praying.

¹¹All at once an angel from the Lord appeared to Zechariah at the right side of the altar. ¹²Zechariah was confused and afraid when he saw the angel. ¹³But the angel told him:

Don't be afraid, Zechariah! God has heard your prayers. Your wife Elizabeth will have a son, and you must name him John. ¹⁴His birth will make you very happy, and many people will be glad. ¹⁵Your son will be a great servant of the Lord. He must never drink wine or beer, and the power of the Holy Spirit will be with him from the time he is born.

¹⁶John will lead many people in Israel to turn back to the Lord their God. ¹⁷He will go ahead of the Lord with the same power and spirit that Elijah* had. And because of John, parents will be more thoughtful of their children. And people who now disobey God will begin to think as they ought to. That is how John will get people ready for the Lord.

¹⁸Zechariah said to the angel, "How will I know this is going to happen? My wife and I are both very old."

¹⁹The angel answered, "I am Gabriel, God's servant, and I was sent to tell you this good news. ²⁰You have not believed what I have said. So you will not be able to say a thing until all this happens. But everything will take place when it is supposed to."

²¹The crowd was waiting for Zechariah and kept wondering why he was staying so long in the temple. ²²When he did come out, he could not speak, and they knew he had seen a vision. He motioned to them with his hands, but did not say a thing.

1.3 a careful study: Or "a study from the beginning".
1.5 Aaron: The brother of Moses and the first priest.

1.9 burn incense: This was done twice a day, in the morning and in the late afternoon.
1.17 Elijah: The prophet Elijah was known for his power to perform miracles.

²³When Zechariah's time of service in the temple was over, he went home. ²⁴Soon after that, his wife was expecting a baby, and for five months she did not leave the house. She said to herself, ²⁵"What the Lord has done for me will keep people from looking down on me."*

An angel tells about the birth of Jesus

²⁶One month later God sent the angel Gabriel to the town of Nazareth in Galilee ²⁷with a message for a virgin named Mary. She was engaged to Joseph from the family of King David. ²⁸The angel greeted Mary and said, "You are truly blessed! The Lord is with you."

²⁹Mary was confused by the angel's words and wondered what they meant. ³⁰Then the angel told Mary, "Don't be afraid! God is pleased with you, ³¹and you will have a son. His name will be Jesus. ³²He will be great and will be called the Son of God Most High. The Lord God will make him king, as his ancestor David was. ³³He will rule the people of Israel for ever, and his kingdom will never end."

³⁴Mary asked the angel, "How can this happen? I am not married!"

³⁵The angel answered, "The Holy Spirit will come down to you, and God's power will come over you. So your child will be called the holy Son of God. ³⁶Your relative Elizabeth is also going to have a son, even though she is old. No one thought she could ever have a baby, but in three months she will have a son. ³⁷Nothing is impossible for God!"

³⁸Mary said, "I am the Lord's servant! Let it happen as you have said." And the angel left her.

Mary visits Elizabeth

³⁹A short time later Mary hurried to a town in the hill country of Judea. ⁴⁰She went into Zechariah's home, where she greeted Elizabeth. ⁴¹When Elizabeth heard Mary's greeting, her baby moved within her.

The Holy Spirit came upon Elizabeth. ⁴²Then in a loud voice she said to Mary:

God has blessed you more than any other woman! He has also blessed the child you will have. ⁴³Why should the mother of my Lord come to me? ⁴⁴As soon as I heard your greeting, my baby became happy and moved within me. ⁴⁵The Lord has blessed you because you believed that he will keep his promise.

Mary's song of praise

⁴⁶Mary said:

With all my heart ⁴⁷I praise the Lord,
and I am glad because of God my Saviour.

1.25 keep people from looking down on me: When a married woman could not have children, it was thought that the Lord was punishing her.

[48]God cares for me, his humble servant.
From now on, all people will say
  God has blessed me.
[49]God All-Powerful has done great things for me,
  and his name is holy.
[50]He always shows mercy
  to everyone who worships him.
[51]The Lord has used his powerful arm
  to scatter those who are proud.
[52]God drags strong rulers from their thrones
  and puts humble people in places of power.
[53]God gives the hungry good things to eat,
and sends the rich away
  with nothing.
[54]God helps his servant Israel
  and is always merciful to his people.
[55]The Lord made this promise to our ancestors,
  to Abraham and his family for ever!

[56]Mary stayed with Elizabeth about three months. Then she went back home.

The birth of John the Baptist

[57]When Elizabeth's son was born, [58]her neighbours and relatives heard how kind the Lord had been to her, and they too were glad.

[59]Eight days later they did for the child what the Law of Moses commands.* They were going to name him Zechariah, after his father. [60]But Elizabeth said, "No! His name is John."

[61]The people argued, "No one in your family has ever been named John."
[62]So they motioned to Zechariah to find out what he wanted to name his son.
[63]Zechariah asked for a writing tablet. Then he wrote, "His name is John." Everyone was amazed. [64]Straight away Zechariah started speaking and praising God.

[65]All the neighbours were frightened because of what had happened, and everywhere in the hill country people kept talking about these things.
[66]Everyone who heard about this wondered what this child would grow up to be. They knew that the Lord was with him.

Zechariah praises the Lord

[67]The Holy Spirit came upon Zechariah, and he began to speak:

[68]Praise the Lord, the God of Israel!
  He has come to save his people.

1.59 what the Law of Moses commands: This refers to circumcision. It is the cutting off of skin from the private part of Jewish boys eight days after birth to show that they belong to the Lord.

⁶⁹Our God has given us a mighty Saviour*
   from the family of David his servant.
⁷⁰Long ago the Lord promised
   by the words of his holy prophets
⁷¹to save us from our enemies
   and from everyone who hates us.
⁷²God said he would be kind to our people
   and keep his sacred promise.
⁷³He told our ancestor Abraham
   ⁷⁴that he would rescue us from our enemies.
Then we could serve him without fear,
   ⁷⁵by being holy and good as long as we live.

⁷⁶You, my son, will be called
   a prophet of God in heaven above.
You will go ahead of the Lord
   to get everything ready for him.
⁷⁷You will tell his people
   that they can be saved when their sins are forgiven.
⁷⁸God's love and kindness will shine upon us
   like the sun that rises in the sky.*
⁷⁹On us who live in the dark shadow of death
this light will shine
   to guide us into a life of peace.

⁸⁰As John grew up, God's Spirit gave him great power. John lived in the desert until the time he was sent to the people of Israel.

The birth of Jesus

2 About that time Emperor Augustus gave orders for the names of all the people to be listed in record books.* ²These first records were made when Quirinius was governor of Syria.*

³Everyone had to go to their own home town to be listed. ⁴So Joseph had to leave Nazareth in Galilee and go to Bethlehem in Judea. Long ago Bethlehem had been King David's home town, and Joseph went there because he was from David's family.

⁵Mary was engaged to Joseph and travelled with him to Bethlehem. She was soon going to have a baby, ⁶and while they were there, ⁷she gave birth

1.69 a mighty Saviour: The Greek text has "a horn of salvation". In the Scriptures animal horns are often a symbol of great strength.
1.78 like the sun that rises in the sky: Or "like the Messiah coming from heaven."
2.1 names…listed in record books: This was done so that everyone could be made to pay taxes to the Emperor.

2.2 Quirinius was governor of Syria: It is known that Quirinius made a record of the people in AD 6 or 7. But the exact date of the record taking that Luke mentions is not known.

to her firstborn* son. She dressed him in baby clothes* and laid him on a bed of hay, because there was no room for them in the inn.

The shepherds

⁸That night in the fields near Bethlehem some shepherds were guarding their sheep. ⁹All at once an angel came down to them from the Lord, and the brightness of the Lord's glory flashed around them. The shepherds were frightened. ¹⁰But the angel said, "Don't be afraid! I have good news for you, which will make everyone happy. ¹¹This very day in King David's home town a Saviour was born for you. He is Christ the Lord. ¹²You will know who he is, because you will find him dressed in baby clothes and lying on a bed of hay."

¹³Suddenly many other angels came down from heaven and joined in praising God. They said:

¹⁴"Praise God in heaven!
   Peace on earth to everyone who pleases God."

¹⁵After the angels had left and gone back to heaven, the shepherds said to each other, "Let's go to Bethlehem and see what the Lord has told us about." ¹⁶They hurried off and found Mary and Joseph, and they saw the baby lying on a bed of hay.

¹⁷When the shepherds saw Jesus, they told his parents what the angel had said about him. ¹⁸Everyone listened and was surprised. ¹⁹But Mary kept thinking about all this and wondering what it meant.

²⁰As the shepherds returned to their sheep, they were praising God and saying wonderful things about him. Everything they had seen and heard was just as the angel had said.

²¹Eight days later Jesus' parents did for him what the Law of Moses commands.* And they named him Jesus, just as the angel had told Mary when he promised she would have a baby.

Simeon praises the Lord

²²The time came for Mary and Joseph to do what the Law of Moses says a mother is supposed to do after her baby is born.*

They took Jesus to the temple in Jerusalem and presented him to the Lord, ²³just as the Law of the Lord says, "Each firstborn* baby boy belongs to the Lord." ²⁴The Law of the Lord also says that parents have to offer a sacrifice, giving at least a pair of doves or two young pigeons. So that is what Mary and Joseph did.

²⁵At this time a man named Simeon was living in Jerusalem. Simeon was a good man. He loved God and was waiting for God to save the people of Israel. God's Spirit came to him ²⁶and told him that he would not die until he had seen Christ the Lord.

²⁷When Mary and Joseph brought Jesus to the temple to do what the Law of Moses says should be done for a new baby, the Spirit told Simeon to go into the temple. ²⁸Simeon took the baby Jesus in his arms and praised God,

²⁹"Lord, I am your servant,
and now I can die in peace,
    because you have kept your promise to me.
³⁰With my own eyes I have seen
what you have done to save your people,
    ³¹and foreign nations will also see this.
³²Your mighty power is a light for all nations,
    and it will bring honour to your people Israel."

³³Jesus' parents were surprised at what Simeon had said. ³⁴Then he blessed them and told Mary, "This child of yours will cause many people in Israel to fall and others to stand. The child will be like a warning sign. Many people will reject him, ³⁵and you, Mary, will suffer as though you had been stabbed by a dagger. But all this will show what people are really thinking."

Anna speaks about the child Jesus

³⁶The prophet Anna was also there in the temple. She was the daughter of Phanuel from the tribe of Asher, and she was very old. In her youth she had been married for seven years, but her husband died. ³⁷And now she was eighty-four years old.* Night and day she served God in the temple by praying and often going without eating.*

³⁸At that time Anna came in and praised God. She spoke about the child Jesus to everyone who hoped for Jerusalem to be set free.

The return to Nazareth

³⁹After Joseph and Mary had done everything that the Law of the Lord commands, they returned home to Nazareth in Galilee. ⁴⁰The child Jesus grew. He became strong and wise, and God blessed him.

The boy Jesus in the temple

⁴¹Every year Jesus' parents went to Jerusalem for Passover. ⁴²And when Jesus was twelve years old, they all went there as usual for the celebration. ⁴³After Passover his parents left, but they did not know that Jesus had stayed on in

2.37 And now she was eighty-four years old: Or "And now she had been a widow for eighty-four years."

2.37 Without eating: The Jewish people sometimes went without eating (also called "fasting") to show their love for God or to show sorrow for their sins.

the city. ⁴⁴They thought he was travelling with some other people, and they went a whole day before they started looking for him. ⁴⁵When they could not find him with their relatives and friends, they went back to Jerusalem and started looking for him there.

⁴⁶Three days later they found Jesus sitting in the temple, listening to the teachers and asking them questions. ⁴⁷Everyone who heard him was surprised at how much he knew and at the answers he gave.

⁴⁸When his parents found him, they were amazed. His mother said, "Son, why have you done this to us? Your father and I have been very worried, and we have been searching for you!"

⁴⁹Jesus answered, "Why did you have to look for me? Didn't you know that I would be in my Father's house?"* ⁵⁰But they did not understand what he meant.

⁵¹Jesus went back to Nazareth with his parents and obeyed them. His mother kept on thinking about all that had happened.

⁵²Jesus became wise, and he grew strong. God was pleased with him and so were the people.

The preaching of John the Baptist

3 For fifteen years* Emperor Tiberius had ruled that part of the world. Pontius Pilate was governor of Judea, and Herod* was the ruler of Galilee. Herod's brother, Philip, was the ruler in the countries of Iturea and Trachonitis, and Lysanias was the ruler of Abilene. ²Annas and Caiaphas were the Jewish high priests.*

At that time God spoke to Zechariah's son John, who was living in the desert. ³So John went along the Jordan Valley, telling the people, "Turn back to God and be baptized! Then your sins will be forgiven." ⁴Isaiah the prophet wrote about John when he said,

"In the desert someone is shouting,
'Get the road ready for the Lord!
    Make a straight path for him.
⁵Fill up every valley and level every mountain and hill.
Straighten the crooked paths
    and smooth out the rough roads.
⁶Then everyone will see the saving power of God.' "

⁷Crowds of people came out to be baptized, but John said to them, "You snakes! Who warned you to run from the coming judgment? ⁸Do something

2.49 in my Father's house: Or "doing my Father's work".
3.1 For fifteen years: This was either AD 28 or 29, and Jesus was about thirty years old (see 3.23).

3.1 Herod: Herod Antipas, the son of Herod the Great.
3.2 Annas and Caiaphas...high priests: Annas was high priest from AD 6 until 15. His son-in-law Caiaphas was high priest from AD 18 until 37.

to show that you really have given up your sins. Don't start saying that you belong to Abraham's family. God can turn these stones into children for Abraham.* [9] An axe is ready to cut the trees down at their roots. Any tree that doesn't produce good fruit will be cut down and thrown into a fire."

[10] The crowds asked John, "What should we do?"

[11] John told them, "If you have two coats, give one to someone who doesn't have any. If you have food, share it with someone else."

[12] When tax collectors* came to be baptized, they asked John, "Teacher, what should we do?"

[13] John told them, "Don't make people pay more than they owe."

[14] Some soldiers asked him, "And what about us? What do we have to do?" John told them, "Don't force people to pay money to make you leave them alone. Be satisfied with your pay."

[15] Everyone became excited and wondered, "Could John be the Messiah?"

[16] John said, "I am just baptizing with water. But someone more powerful is going to come, and I am not good enough even to untie his sandals.* He will baptize you with the Holy Spirit and with fire. [17] His threshing fork* is in his hand, and he is ready to separate the wheat from the husks. He will store the wheat in his barn and burn the husks with a fire that never goes out."

[18] In many different ways John preached the good news to the people. [19] But to Herod the ruler, he said, "It was wrong for you to take Herodias, your brother's wife." John also said that Herod had done many other bad things. [20] Finally, Herod put John in jail, and this was the worst thing he had done.

The baptism of Jesus

[21] While everyone else was being baptized, Jesus himself was baptized. Then as he prayed, the sky opened up, [22] and the Holy Spirit came down upon him in the form of a dove. A voice from heaven said, "You are my own dear Son, and I am pleased with you."

The ancestors of Jesus

[23] When Jesus began to preach, he was about thirty years old. Everyone thought he was the son of Joseph. But his family went back through Heli, [24] Matthat, Levi, Melchi, Jannai, Joseph, [25] Mattathias, Amos, Nahum, Esli, Naggai, [26] Maath, Mattathias, Semein, Josech, Joda;

3.8 children for Abraham: The Jewish people thought they were God's chosen people because of God's promises to their ancestor Abraham.
3.12 tax collectors: These were usually Jewish people who paid the Romans for the right to collect taxes. They were hated by other Jews who thought of them as traitors to their country and to their religion.

3.16 untie his sandals: This was the duty of a slave.
3.17 threshing fork: After Jewish farmers had trampled out the grain, they used a large fork to pitch the grain and the husks into the air. Wind would blow away the light husks, and the grain would fall back to the ground, where it could be gathered up.

27Joanan, Rhesa, Zerubbabel, Shealtiel, Neri, 28Melchi, Addi, Cosam, Elmadam, Er, 29Joshua, Eliezer, Jorim, Matthat, Levi;

30Simeon, Judah, Joseph, Jonam, Eliakim, 31Melea, Menna, Mattatha, Nathan, David, 32Jesse, Obed, Boaz, Salmon, Nahshon;

33Amminadab, Admin, Arni, Hezron, Perez, Judah, 34Jacob, Isaac, Abraham, Terah, Nahor, 35Serug, Reu, Peleg, Eber, Shelah;

36Cainan, Arphaxad, Shem, Noah, Lamech, 37Methuselah, Enoch, Jared, Mahalaleel, Kenan, 38Enosh, and Seth.

The family of Jesus went all the way back to Adam and then to God.

Jesus and the devil

4 When Jesus returned from the River Jordan, the power of the Holy Spirit was with him, and the Spirit led him into the desert. 2For forty days Jesus was tested by the devil, and during that time he went without eating.* When it was all over, he was hungry.

3The devil said to Jesus, "If you are God's Son, tell this stone to turn into bread."

4Jesus answered, "The Scriptures say, 'No one can live only on food.' "

5Then the devil led Jesus up to a high place and quickly showed him all the nations on earth. 6The devil said, "I will give all this power and glory to you. It has been given to me, and I can give it to anyone I want to. 7Just worship me, and you can have it all."

8Jesus answered, "The Scriptures say:

'Worship the Lord your God
 and serve only him!' "

9Finally, the devil took Jesus to Jerusalem and had him stand on top of the temple. The devil said, "If you are God's Son, jump off. 10-11The Scriptures say:

'God will tell his angels to take care of you.
 They will catch you in their arms,
  and you will not hurt your feet on the stones.' "

12Jesus answered, "The Scriptures also say, 'Don't try to test the Lord your God!' "

13After the devil had finished testing Jesus in every way possible, he left him for a while.

Jesus begins his work

14Jesus returned to Galilee with the power of the Spirit. News about him spread everywhere. 15He taught in the Jewish meeting places, and everyone praised him.

4.2 went without eating: See the note at 2.37.

The people of Nazareth turn against Jesus

[16]Jesus went back to Nazareth, where he had been brought up, and as usual he went to the meeting place on the Sabbath. When he stood up to read from the Scriptures, [17]he was given the book of Isaiah the prophet. He opened it and read,

[18]"The Lord's Spirit has come to me,
because he has chosen me
    to tell the good news to the poor.
The Lord has sent me to announce freedom for prisoners,
to give sight to the blind, to free everyone who suffers,
[19]and to say, 'This is the year the Lord has chosen.' "

[20]Jesus closed the book, then handed it back to the man in charge and sat down. Everyone in the meeting place looked straight at Jesus.

[21]Then Jesus said to them, "What you have just heard me read has come true today."

[22]All the people started talking about Jesus and were amazed at the wonderful things he said. They kept on asking, "Isn't he Joseph's son?"

[23]Jesus answered:

You will certainly want to tell me this saying, "Doctor, first make yourself well." You will tell me to do the same things here in my own home town that you heard I did in Capernaum. [24]But you can be sure that no prophets are liked by the people of their own home town.

[25]Once during the time of Elijah there was no rain for three and a half years, and people everywhere were starving. There were many widows in Israel, [26]but Elijah was sent only to a widow in the town of Zarephath near the city of Sidon. [27]During the time of the prophet Elisha, many men in Israel had leprosy.* But no one was healed, except Naaman who lived in Syria.

[28]When the people in the meeting place heard Jesus say this, they became so angry [29]that they got up and threw him out of town. They dragged him to the edge of the cliff on which the town was built, because they wanted to throw him down from there. [30]But Jesus slipped through the crowd and got away.

A man with an evil spirit

[31]Jesus went to the town of Capernaum in Galilee and taught the people on the Sabbath. [32]His teaching amazed them because he spoke with power. [33]There in the Jewish meeting place was a man with an evil spirit. He yelled out, [34]"Hey, Jesus of Nazareth, what do you want with us? Are you here to get rid of us? I know who you are! You are God's Holy One."

4.27 leprosy: In biblical times the word "leprosy" was used for many different kinds of skin diseases.

[35]Jesus ordered the evil spirit to be quiet and come out. The demon threw the man to the ground in front of everyone and left without harming him.

[36]They all were amazed and kept saying to each other, "What kind of teaching is this? He has power to order evil spirits out of people!" [37]News about Jesus spread all over that part of the country.

Jesus heals many people

[38]Jesus left the meeting place and went to Simon's home. When Jesus got there, he was told that Simon's mother-in-law was sick with a high fever. [39]So Jesus went over to her and ordered the fever to go away. At once she was able to get up and serve them a meal.

[40]After the sun had set, people with all kinds of diseases were brought to Jesus. He put his hands on each one of them and healed them. [41]Demons went out of many people and shouted, "You are the Son of God!" But Jesus ordered the demons not to speak because they knew he was the Messiah.

[42]The next morning Jesus went out to a place where he could be alone, and crowds came looking for him. When they found him, they tried to stop him from leaving. [43]But Jesus said, "People in other towns must hear the good news about God's kingdom. That's why I was sent." [44]So he kept on preaching in the Jewish meeting places in Judea.*

Jesus chooses his first disciples

5 Jesus was standing on the shore of Lake Gennesaret,* teaching the people as they crowded around him to hear God's message. [2]Near the shore he saw two boats left there by some fishermen who had gone to wash their nets. [3]Jesus got into the boat that belonged to Simon and asked him to row it out a little way from the shore. Then Jesus sat down* in the boat to teach the crowd.

[4]When Jesus had finished speaking, he told Simon, "Row the boat out into the deep water and let your nets down to catch some fish."

[5]"Master," Simon answered, "we have worked hard all night long and have not caught a thing. But if you tell me to, I will let the nets down." [6]They did it and caught so many fish that their nets began ripping apart. [7]Then they signalled for their partners in the other boat to come and help them. The men came, and together they filled the two boats so full that they both began to sink.

[8]When Simon Peter saw this happen, he knelt down in front of Jesus and said, "Lord, don't come near me! I am a sinner." [9]Peter and everyone with him were completely surprised at all the fish they had caught. [10]His partners James and John, the sons of Zebedee, were surprised too.

4.44 Judea: Some manuscripts have "Galilee".
5.1 Lake Gennesaret: Another name for Lake Galilee.

5.3 sat down: Teachers in the ancient world, including Jewish teachers, usually sat down when they taught.

Jesus told Simon, "Don't be afraid! From now on you will bring in people instead of fish." ¹¹The men pulled their boats up on the shore. Then they left everything and went with Jesus.

Jesus heals a man

¹²Jesus came to a town where there was a man who had leprosy.* When the man saw Jesus, he knelt down on the ground in front of Jesus and begged, "Lord, you have the power to make me well, if only you wanted to."

¹³Jesus put his hand on him and said, "I want to! Now you are well." At once the man's leprosy disappeared. ¹⁴Jesus told him, "Don't tell anyone about this, but go and show yourself to the priest. Offer a gift to the priest, just as Moses commanded, and everyone will know that you have been healed."*

¹⁵News about Jesus kept spreading. Large crowds came to listen to him teach and to be healed of their diseases. ¹⁶But Jesus would often go to some place where he could be alone and pray.

Jesus heals a crippled man

¹⁷One day some Pharisees and experts in the Law of Moses sat listening to Jesus teach. They had come from every village in Galilee and Judea and from Jerusalem.

God had given Jesus the power to heal the sick, ¹⁸and some people came carrying a crippled man on a mat. They tried to take him inside the house and put him in front of Jesus. ¹⁹But because of the crowd, they could not get him to Jesus. So they went up on the roof,* where they removed some tiles and let the mat down in the middle of the room.

²⁰When Jesus saw how much faith they had, he said to the crippled man, "My friend, your sins are forgiven."

²¹The Pharisees and the experts began arguing, "Jesus must think he is God! Only God can forgive sins."

²²Jesus knew what they were thinking, and he said, "Why are you thinking that? ²³Is it easier for me to tell this crippled man that his sins are forgiven or to tell him to get up and walk? ²⁴But now you will see that the Son of Man has the right to forgive sins here on earth." Jesus then said to the man, "Get up! Pick up your mat and walk home."

5.12 leprosy: See the note at 4.27.
5.14 everyone will know that you have been healed: People with leprosy had to be examined by a priest and told that they were well (that is, "clean") before they could once again live a normal life in the Jewish community. The gift that Moses commanded was the sacrifice of some lambs together with flour mixed with olive oil.

5.19 roof: In Palestine the houses usually had a flat roof. Stairs on the outside led up to the roof, which was made of beams and boards covered with packed earth. Luke says that the roof was made of (clay) tiles, which were also used for making roofs in New Testament times.

²⁵At once the man stood up in front of everyone. He picked up his mat and went home, giving thanks to God. ²⁶Everyone was amazed and praised God. What they saw surprised them, and they said, "We have seen a great miracle today!"

Jesus chooses Levi

²⁷Later, Jesus went out and saw a tax collector* named Levi sitting at the place for paying taxes. Jesus said to him, "Come with me." ²⁸Levi left everything and went with Jesus.

²⁹In his home Levi gave a big dinner for Jesus. Many tax collectors and other guests were also there.

³⁰The Pharisees and some of their teachers of the Law of Moses grumbled to Jesus' disciples, "Why do you eat and drink with those tax collectors and other sinners?"

³¹Jesus answered, "Healthy people don't need a doctor, but sick people do. ³²I didn't come to invite good people to turn to God. I came to invite sinners."

People ask about going without eating

³³Some people said to Jesus, "John's followers often pray and go without eating,* and so do the followers of the Pharisees. But your disciples never go without eating or drinking."

³⁴Jesus told them, "The friends of a bridegroom don't go without eating while he is still with them. ³⁵But the time will come when he will be taken from them. Then they will go without eating."

³⁶Jesus then told them these sayings:

No one uses a new piece of cloth to patch old clothes. The patch would shrink and make the hole even bigger.

³⁷No one pours new wine into old wineskins. The new wine would swell and burst the old skins.* Then the wine would be lost, and the skins would be ruined. ³⁸New wine must be put only into new wineskins.

³⁹No one wants new wine after drinking old wine. They say, "The old wine is better."

A question about the Sabbath

6 One Sabbath when Jesus and his disciples were walking through some wheat fields,* the disciples picked some wheat. They rubbed the husks off with their hands and started eating the grain.

5.27 **tax collector:** See the note at 3.12.
5.33 **without eating:** See the note at 2.37.
5.37 **swell and burst the old skins:** While the juice from grapes was becoming wine, it would swell and stretch the skins in which it had been stored. If the skins were old and stiff, they would burst.

6.1 **walking through some wheat fields:** It was the custom to let hungry travellers pick grains of wheat.

²Some Pharisees said, "Why are you picking grain on the Sabbath? You're not supposed to do that!"

³Jesus answered, "You surely have read what David did when he and his followers were hungry. ⁴He went into the house of God and took the sacred loaves of bread that only priests were supposed to eat. He not only ate some himself, but even gave some to his followers."

⁵Jesus finished by saying, "The Son of Man is Lord over the Sabbath."

A man with a crippled hand

⁶On another Sabbath* Jesus was teaching in a Jewish meeting place, and a man with a crippled right hand was there. ⁷Some Pharisees and teachers of the Law of Moses kept watching Jesus to see if he would heal the man. They did this because they wanted to accuse Jesus of doing something wrong.

⁸Jesus knew what they were thinking. So he told the man to stand up where everyone could see him. And the man stood up. ⁹Then Jesus asked, "On the Sabbath should we do good deeds or evil deeds? Should we save someone's life or destroy it?"

¹⁰After he had looked around at everyone, he told the man, "Stretch out your hand." He did, and his bad hand became completely well.

¹¹The teachers and the Pharisees were furious and started saying to each other, "What can we do about Jesus?"

Jesus chooses his twelve apostles

¹²About that time Jesus went off to a mountain to pray, and he spent the whole night there. ¹³The next morning he called his disciples together and chose twelve of them to be his apostles. ¹⁴One was Simon, and Jesus named him Peter. Another was Andrew, Peter's brother. There were also James, John, Philip, Bartholomew, ¹⁵Matthew, Thomas, and James the son of Alphaeus. The rest of the apostles were Simon, known as the Eager One,* ¹⁶Jude, who was the son of James, and Judas Iscariot,* who later betrayed Jesus.

Jesus teaches, preaches, and heals

¹⁷Jesus and his apostles went down from the mountain and came to some flat, level ground. Many other disciples were there to meet him. Large

6.6 On another Sabbath: Some manuscripts have a reading which may mean "the Sabbath after the next".
6.15 known as the Eager One: The word "eager" translates the Greek word "zealot", which was a name later given to the members of a Jewish group that resisted and fought against the Romans.

6.16 Iscariot: This may mean "a man from Kerioth" (a place in Judea). But more probably it means "a man who was a liar" or "a man who was a betrayer".

crowds of people from all over Judea, Jerusalem, and the coastal cities of Tyre and Sidon were there too. ¹⁸These people had come to listen to Jesus and to be healed of their diseases. All who were troubled by evil spirits were also healed. ¹⁹Everyone was trying to touch Jesus, because power was going out from him and healing them all.

Blessings and troubles

²⁰Jesus looked at his disciples and said:

God will bless you people who are poor.
  His kingdom belongs to you!
²¹God will bless you hungry people.
  You will have plenty to eat!
God will bless you people who are crying.
  You will laugh!

²²God will bless you when others hate you and won't have anything to do with you. God will bless you when people insult you and say cruel things about you, all because you are a follower of the Son of Man. ²³Long ago your own people did these same things to the prophets. So when this happens to you, be happy and jump for joy! You will have a great reward in heaven.

²⁴But you rich people are in for trouble.
  You have already had an easy life!
²⁵You well-fed people are in for trouble.
  You will go hungry!
You people who are laughing now are in for trouble.
  You are going to cry and weep!

²⁶You are in for trouble when everyone says good things about you. That is what your own people said about those prophets who told lies.

Love for enemies

Jesus continued:

²⁷This is what I say to all who will listen to me:

Love your enemies, and be good to everyone who hates you. ²⁸Ask God to bless anyone who curses you, and pray for everyone who is cruel to you. ²⁹If someone slaps you on one cheek, don't stop that person from slapping you on the other cheek. If someone wants to take your coat, don't try to keep back your shirt. ³⁰Give to everyone who asks and don't ask people to return what they have taken from you. ³¹Treat others just as you want to be treated.

³²If you love only someone who loves you, will God praise you for that? Even sinners love people who love them. ³³If you are kind only to someone who is kind to you, will God be pleased with you for that? Even sinners are kind to people who are kind to them. ³⁴If you lend money only to someone you think will pay you back, will God be pleased with you for that? Even sinners lend to sinners because they think they will get it all back.

³⁵But love your enemies and be good to them. Lend without expecting to be paid back.* Then you will get a great reward, and you will be the true children of God in heaven. He is good even to people who are unthankful and cruel. ³⁶Have pity on others, just as your Father has pity on you.

Judging others

³⁷Jesus said:

Don't judge others, and God won't judge you. Don't be hard on others, and God won't be hard on you. Forgive others, and God will forgive you. ³⁸If you give to others, you will be given a full amount in return. It will be packed down, shaken together, and spilling over into your lap. The way you treat others is the way you will be treated.

³⁹Jesus also used some sayings as he spoke to the people. He said:

Can one blind person lead another blind person? Won't they both fall into a ditch? ⁴⁰Are students better than their teacher? But when they are fully trained, they will be like their teacher.

⁴¹You can see the speck in your friend's eye. But you don't notice the log in your own eye. ⁴²How can you say, "My friend, let me take the speck out of your eye," when you don't see the log in your own eye? You show-offs! First, get the log out of your own eye. Then you can see how to take the speck out of your friend's eye.

A tree and its fruit

Jesus continued:

⁴³A good tree cannot produce bad fruit, and a bad tree cannot produce good fruit. ⁴⁴You can tell what a tree is like by the fruit it produces. You cannot pick figs or grapes from thorn bushes. ⁴⁵Good people do good things because of the good in their hearts. Bad people do bad things because of the evil in their hearts. Your words show what is in your heart.

6.35 without expecting to be paid back:
Some manuscripts have "without giving up on anyone".

16 :

Two builders

Jesus continued:

⁴⁶Why do you keep on saying that I am your Lord, when you refuse to do what I say? ⁴⁷Anyone who comes and listens to me and obeys me ⁴⁸is like someone who dug down deep and built a house on solid rock. When the flood came and the river rushed against the house, it was built so well that it didn't even shake. ⁴⁹But anyone who hears what I say and doesn't obey me is like someone whose house wasn't built on solid rock. As soon as the river rushed against that house, it was smashed to pieces!

Jesus heals an army officer's servant

7 After Jesus had finished teaching the people, he went to Capernaum. ²In that town an army officer's servant was sick and about to die. The officer liked this servant very much. ³And when he heard about Jesus, he sent some Jewish leaders to ask him to come and heal the servant.

⁴The leaders went to Jesus and begged him to do something. They said, "This man deserves your help! ⁵He loves our nation and even built us a meeting place." ⁶So Jesus went with them.

When Jesus wasn't far from the house, the officer sent some friends to tell him, "Lord, don't go to any trouble for me! I am not good enough for you to come into my house. ⁷And I am certainly not worthy to come to you. Just say the word, and my servant will get well. ⁸I have officers who give orders to me, and I have soldiers who take orders from me. I can say to one of them, 'Go!' and he goes. I can say to another, 'Come!' and he comes. I can say to my servant, 'Do this!' and he will do it."

⁹When Jesus heard this, he was so surprised that he turned and said to the crowd following him, "In all of Israel I've never found anyone with this much faith!"

¹⁰The officer's friends returned and found the servant well.

A widow's son

¹¹Soon Jesus and his disciples were on their way to the town of Nain, and a big crowd was going along with them. ¹²As they came near the gate of the town, they saw people carrying out the body of a widow's only son. Many people from the town were walking along with her.

¹³When the Lord saw the woman, he felt sorry for her and said, "Don't cry!"

¹⁴Jesus went over and touched the stretcher on which the people were carrying the dead boy. They stopped, and Jesus said, "Young man, get up!" ¹⁵The boy sat up and began to speak. Jesus then gave him back to his mother.

¹⁶Everyone was frightened and praised God. They said, "A great prophet is here with us! God has come to his people."

¹⁷News about Jesus spread all over Judea and everywhere else in that part of the country.

John the Baptist

¹⁸⁻¹⁹John's followers told John everything that was being said about Jesus. So he sent two of them to ask the Lord, "Are you the one we should be looking for? Or must we wait for someone else?"

²⁰When these messengers came to Jesus, they said, "John the Baptist sent us to ask, 'Are you the one we should be looking for? Or are we supposed to wait for someone else?' "

²¹At that time Jesus was healing many people who were sick or in pain or were troubled by evil spirits, and he was giving sight to a lot of blind people. ²²Jesus said to the messengers sent by John, "Go and tell John what you have seen and heard. Blind people are now able to see, and the lame can walk. People who have leprosy* are being healed, and the deaf can now hear. The dead are raised to life, and the poor are hearing the good news. ²³God will bless everyone who doesn't reject me because of what I do."

²⁴After John's messengers had gone, Jesus began speaking to the crowds about John:

What kind of person did you go out to the desert to see? Was he like tall grass blown about by the wind? ²⁵What kind of man did you really go out to see? Was he someone dressed in fine clothes? People who wear expensive clothes and live in luxury are in the king's palace. ²⁶What then did you go out to see? Was he a prophet? He certainly was! I tell you that he was more than a prophet. ²⁷In the Scriptures, God calls John his messenger and says, "I am sending my messenger ahead of you to get things ready for you." ²⁸No one ever born on this earth is greater than John. But whoever is least important in God's kingdom is greater than John.

²⁹Everyone had been listening to John. Even the tax collectors* had obeyed God and had done what was right by letting John baptize them. ³⁰But the Pharisees and the experts in the Law of Moses refused to obey God and be baptized by John.

³¹Jesus went on to say:

What are you people like? What kind of people are you? ³²You are like children sitting in the market and shouting to each other,

"We played the flute, but you would not dance!
We sang a funeral song, but you would not cry!"

---

18 : **7.22 leprosy:** See the note at 4.27.   **7.29 tax collectors:** See the note at 3.12.

[33]John the Baptist did not go around eating and drinking, and you said, "John has a demon in him!" [34]But because the Son of Man goes around eating and drinking, you say, "Jesus eats and drinks too much! He is even a friend of tax collectors and sinners." [35]Yet Wisdom is shown to be right by what its followers do.

Simon the Pharisee

[36]A Pharisee invited Jesus to have dinner with him. So Jesus went to the Pharisee's home and got ready to eat.*

[37]When a sinful woman in that town found out that Jesus was there, she bought an expensive bottle of perfume. [38]Then she came and stood behind Jesus. She cried and started washing his feet with her tears and drying them with her hair. The woman kissed his feet and poured the perfume on them.

[39]The Pharisee who had invited Jesus saw this and said to himself, "If this man really were a prophet, he would know what kind of woman is touching him! He would know that she is a sinner."

[40]Jesus said to the Pharisee, "Simon, I have something to say to you."

"Teacher, what is it?" Simon replied.

[41]Jesus told him, "Two people were in debt to a moneylender. One of them owed him five hundred silver coins, and the other owed him fifty. [42]Since neither of them could pay him back, the moneylender said that they didn't have to pay him anything. Which one of them will like him more?"

[43]Simon answered, "I suppose it would be the one who had owed more and didn't have to pay it back."

"You are right," Jesus said.

[44]He turned towards the woman and said to Simon, "Have you noticed this woman? When I came into your home, you didn't give me any water so I could wash my feet. But she has washed my feet with her tears and dried them with her hair. [45]You didn't greet me with a kiss, but from the time I came in, she has not stopped kissing my feet. [46]You didn't even pour olive oil on my head,* but she has poured expensive perfume on my feet. [47]So I tell you that all her sins are forgiven, and that is why she has shown great love. But anyone who has been forgiven for only a little will show only a little love."

[48]Then Jesus said to the woman, "Your sins are forgiven."

[49]Some other guests started saying to one another, "Who is this who dares to forgive sins?"

7.36 got ready to eat: On special occasions the Jewish people often followed the Greek and Roman custom of lying down on their left side and leaning on their left elbow, while eating with their right hand. This is how the woman could come up behind Jesus and wash his feet (see verse 38).

7.44, 46 washed my feet...greet me with a kiss...pour olive oil on my head: Guests in a home were usually offered water so they could wash their feet, because most people either went barefoot or wore sandals and would come into the house with very dusty feet. Guests were also greeted with a kiss on the cheek, and special ones often had sweet-smelling olive oil poured on their head.

⁵⁰But Jesus told the woman, "Because of your faith, you are now saved.*
May God give you peace!"

Women who helped Jesus

8 Soon after this, Jesus was going through towns and villages, telling the good news about God's kingdom. His twelve apostles were with him, ²and so were some women who had been healed of evil spirits and all sorts of diseases. One of the women was Mary Magdalene,* who once had seven demons in her. ³Joanna, Susanna, and many others had also used what they owned to help Jesus* and his disciples. Joanna's husband Chuza was one of Herod's officials.*

A story about a farmer

⁴When a large crowd from several towns had gathered around Jesus, he told them this story:

⁵A farmer went out to scatter seed in a field. While the farmer was doing it, some of the seeds fell along the road and were stepped on or eaten by birds. ⁶Other seeds fell on rocky ground and started growing. But the plants did not have enough water and soon dried up. ⁷Some other seeds fell where thorn bushes grew up and choked the plants. ⁸The rest of the seeds fell on good ground where they grew and produced a hundred times as many seeds.

When Jesus had finished speaking, he said, "If you have ears, pay attention!"

Why Jesus used stories

⁹Jesus' disciples asked him what the story meant. ¹⁰So he answered:

I have explained the secrets about God's kingdom to you, but for others I can only use stories. These people look, but they don't see, and they hear, but they don't understand.

Jesus explains the story about a farmer

¹¹This is what the story means: The seed is God's message, ¹²and the seeds that fell along the road are the people who hear the message. But the devil comes and snatches the message out of their hearts, so that they will not believe and be saved. ¹³The seeds that fell on rocky ground are the people who gladly hear the message and accept it. But they don't have deep roots, and they believe only for a little while. As soon as life gets hard, they give up.

7.50 saved: Or "healed". The Greek word may have either meaning.
8.2 Magdalene: Meaning "from Magdala", a small town on the western shore of Lake Galilee. There is no hint that she is the sinful woman in 7.36–50.

8.3 used what they owned to help Jesus: Women often helped Jewish teachers by giving them money.
8.3 Herod's officials: Herod Antipas, the son of Herod the Great.

¹⁴The seeds that fell among the thorn bushes are also people who hear the message. But they are so eager for riches and pleasures that they never produce anything. ¹⁵Those seeds that fell on good ground are the people who listen to the message and keep it in good and honest hearts. They last and produce a harvest.

Light
Jesus continued:

¹⁶No one lights a lamp and puts it under a bowl or under a bed. A lamp is always put on a lampstand, so that people who come into a house will see the light. ¹⁷There is nothing hidden that will not be found. There is no secret that will not be well known. ¹⁸Pay attention to how you listen! Everyone who has something will be given more, but people who have nothing will lose what little they think they have.

Jesus' mother and brothers

¹⁹Jesus' mother and brothers went to see him, but because of the crowd they could not get near him. ²⁰Someone told Jesus, "Your mother and brothers are standing outside and want to see you."

²¹Jesus answered, "My mother and my brothers are those people who hear and obey God's message."

A storm

²²One day, Jesus and his disciples got into a boat, and he said, "Let's cross the lake."* They started out, ²³and while they were sailing across, he went to sleep.

Suddenly a storm struck the lake, and the boat started sinking. They were in danger. ²⁴So they went to Jesus and woke him up, "Master, Master! We are about to drown!"

Jesus got up and ordered the wind and waves to stop. They obeyed, and everything was calm. ²⁵Then Jesus asked the disciples, "Don't you have any faith?"

But they were frightened and amazed. They said to each other, "Who is this? He can give orders to the wind and the waves, and they obey him!"

A man with demons in him

²⁶Jesus and his disciples sailed across Lake Galilee and came to shore near the town of Gerasa.* ²⁷As Jesus was getting out of the boat, he was met by a man from that town. The man had demons in him. He had gone naked for a long time and no longer lived in a house, but in the graveyard.*

8.22 cross the lake: To the eastern shore of Lake Galilee, where most of the people were not Jewish.

8.26 Gerasa: Some manuscripts have "Gergesa".
8.27 graveyard: It was thought that demons and evil spirits lived in graveyards.

²⁸The man saw Jesus and screamed. He knelt down in front of him and shouted, "Jesus, Son of God in heaven, what do you want with me? I beg you not to torture me!" ²⁹He said this because Jesus had already told the evil spirit to go out of him.

The man had often been attacked by the demon. And even though he had been bound with chains and leg irons and kept under guard, he smashed whatever bound him. Then the demon would force him out into lonely places.

³⁰Jesus asked the man, "What is your name?"

He answered, "My name is Lots." He said this because there were 'lots' of demons in him. ³¹They begged Jesus not to send them to the deep pit,* where they would be punished.

³²A large herd of pigs was feeding there on the hillside. So the demons begged Jesus to let them go into the pigs, and Jesus let them go. ³³Then the demons left the man and went into the pigs. The whole herd rushed down the steep bank into the lake and drowned.

³⁴When the men taking care of the pigs saw this, they ran to spread the news in the town and on the farms. ³⁵The people went out to see what had happened, and when they came to Jesus, they also found the man. The demons had gone out of him, and he was sitting there at the feet of Jesus. He had clothes on and was in his right mind. But the people were terrified.

³⁶Then all who had seen the man healed told about it. ³⁷Everyone from around Gerasa* begged Jesus to leave, because they were so frightened.

When Jesus got into the boat to start back, ³⁸the man who had been healed begged to go with him. But Jesus sent him off and said, ³⁹"Go back home and tell everyone how much God has done for you." The man then went all over town, telling everything that Jesus had done for him.

A dying girl and a sick woman

⁴⁰Everyone had been waiting for Jesus, and when he came back, a crowd was there to welcome him. ⁴¹Just then the man in charge of the Jewish meeting place came and knelt down in front of Jesus. His name was Jairus, and he begged Jesus to come to his home ⁴²because his twelve-year-old child was dying. She was his only daughter.

While Jesus was on his way, people were crowding all around him. ⁴³In the crowd was a woman who had been bleeding for twelve years. She had spent everything she had on doctors,* but none of them could make her well.

⁴⁴As soon as she came up behind Jesus and barely touched his clothes, her bleeding stopped.

8.31 deep pit: The place where evil spirits are kept and punished.

8.37 Gerasa: See the note at 8.26.

8.43 She had spent everything she had on doctors: Some manuscripts do not have these words.

⁴⁵"Who touched me?" Jesus asked.

While everyone was denying it, Peter said, "Master, people are crowding all around and pushing you from every side."*

⁴⁶But Jesus answered, "Someone touched me, because I felt power going out from me." ⁴⁷The woman knew that she could not hide, so she came trembling and knelt down in front of Jesus. She told everyone why she had touched him and that she had been healed straight away.

⁴⁸Jesus said to the woman, "You are now well because of your faith. May God give you peace!"

⁴⁹While Jesus was speaking, someone came from Jairus' home and said, "Your daughter has died! Why bother the teacher any more?"

⁵⁰When Jesus heard this, he told Jairus, "Don't worry! Have faith, and your daughter will get well."

⁵¹Jesus went into the house, but he did not let anyone else go with him, except Peter, John, James, and the girl's father and mother. ⁵²Everyone was crying and weeping for the girl. But Jesus said, "The child isn't dead. She is just asleep." ⁵³The people laughed at him because they knew she was dead.

⁵⁴Jesus took hold of the girl's hand and said, "Child, get up!" ⁵⁵She came back to life and got straight up. Jesus told them to give her something to eat. ⁵⁶Her parents were surprised, but Jesus ordered them not to tell anyone what had happened.

Instructions for the twelve apostles

9 Jesus called together his twelve apostles and gave them complete power over all demons and diseases. ²Then he sent them to tell about God's kingdom and to heal the sick. ³He told them, "Don't take anything with you! Don't take a walking stick or a travelling bag or food or money or even a change of clothes. ⁴When you are welcomed into a home, stay there until you leave that town. ⁵If people won't welcome you, leave the town and shake the dust from your feet* as a warning to them."

⁶The apostles left and went from village to village, telling the good news and healing people everywhere.

Herod is worried

⁷Herod* the ruler heard about all that was happening, and he was worried. Some people were saying that John the Baptist had come back to life. ⁸Others were saying that Elijah had come* or that one of the prophets from

---

8.45 from every side: Some manuscripts add "and you ask, 'Who touched me?'"
9.5 shake the dust from your feet: This was a way of showing rejection.

9.7 Herod: Herod Antipas, the son of Herod the Great.
9.8 Elijah had come: Many of the Jewish people expected the prophet Elijah to come and prepare the way for the Messiah.

long ago had come back to life. ⁹But Herod said, "I had John's head cut off! Who is this I hear so much about?" Herod was eager to meet Jesus.

Jesus feeds five thousand

¹⁰The apostles came back and told Jesus everything they had done. He then took them with him to the village of Bethsaida, where they could be alone. ¹¹But a lot of people found out about this and followed him. Jesus welcomed them. He spoke to them about God's kingdom and healed everyone who was sick.

¹²Late in the afternoon the twelve apostles came to Jesus and said, "Send the crowd to the villages and farms around here. They need to find a place to stay and something to eat. There is nothing in this place. It is like a desert!"

¹³Jesus answered, "You give them something to eat."

But they replied, "We have only five small loaves of bread* and two fish. If we are going to feed all these people, we will have to go and buy food." ¹⁴There were about five thousand men in the crowd.

Jesus said to his disciples, "Have the people sit in groups of fifty." ¹⁵They did this, and all the people sat down. ¹⁶Jesus took the five loaves and the two fish. He looked up towards heaven and blessed the food. Then he broke the bread and fish and handed them to his disciples to give to the people.

¹⁷Everyone ate all they wanted. What was left over filled twelve baskets.

Who is Jesus?

¹⁸When Jesus was alone praying, his disciples came to him, and he asked them, "What do people say about me?"

¹⁹They answered, "Some say that you are John the Baptist or Elijah* or a prophet from long ago who has come back to life."

²⁰Jesus then asked them, "But who do you say I am?"

Peter answered, "You are the Messiah sent from God."

²¹Jesus strictly warned his disciples not to tell anyone about this.

Jesus speaks about his suffering and death

²²Jesus told his disciples, "The nation's leaders, the chief priests, and the teachers of the Law of Moses will make the Son of Man suffer terribly. They will reject him and kill him, but three days later he will rise to life."

²³Then Jesus said to all the people:

If any of you want to be my followers, you must forget about yourself. You must take up your cross each day and follow me. ²⁴If you want to save your life,* you will destroy it. But if you give up your life for me, you

---

9.13 small loaves of bread: These would have been flat and round or in the shape of a bun.

9.19 Elijah: See the note at 9.8.
9.24 life: In verses 24, 25 a Greek word which often means "soul" is translated "life" and "yourself".

will save it. ²⁵What will you gain, if you own the whole world but destroy yourself or waste your life? ²⁶If you are ashamed of me and my message, the Son of Man will be ashamed of you when he comes in his glory and in the glory of his Father and the holy angels. ²⁷You can be sure that some of the people standing here will not die before they see God's kingdom.

The true glory of Jesus

²⁸About eight days later Jesus took Peter, John, and James with him and went up on a mountain to pray. ²⁹While he was praying, his face changed, and his clothes became shining white. ³⁰Suddenly Moses and Elijah were there speaking with him. ³¹They appeared in heavenly glory and talked about all that Jesus' death* in Jerusalem would mean.

³²Peter and the other two disciples had been sound asleep. All at once they woke up and saw how glorious Jesus was. They also saw the two men who were with him.

³³Moses and Elijah were about to leave, when Peter said to Jesus, "Master, it is good for us to be here! Let us make three shelters, one for you, one for Moses, and one for Elijah." But Peter did not know what he was talking about.

³⁴While Peter was still speaking, a shadow from a cloud passed over them, and they were frightened as the cloud covered them. ³⁵From the cloud a voice spoke, "This is my chosen Son. Listen to what he says!"

³⁶After the voice had spoken, Peter, John, and James saw only Jesus. For some time they kept quiet and did not say anything about what they had seen.

Jesus heals a boy

³⁷The next day Jesus and his three disciples came down from the mountain and were met by a large crowd. ³⁸Just then someone in the crowd shouted, "Teacher, please do something for my son! He is my only child! ³⁹A demon often attacks him and makes him scream. It shakes him until he foams at the mouth, and it won't leave him until it has completely worn the boy out. ⁴⁰I begged your disciples to force out the demon, but they couldn't do it."

⁴¹Jesus said to them, "You people are stubborn and don't have any faith! How much longer must I be with you? Why do I have to put up with you?"

Then Jesus said to the man, "Bring your son to me." ⁴²While the boy was being brought, the demon attacked him and made him shake all over. Jesus ordered the demon to stop. Then he healed the boy and gave him back to his father. ⁴³Everyone was amazed at God's great power.

9.31 Jesus' death: In Greek this is "his departure", which probably includes his rising to life and his return to heaven.

Jesus again speaks about his death

While everyone was still amazed at what Jesus was doing, he said to his disciples, ⁴⁴"Pay close attention to what I am telling you! The Son of Man will be handed over to his enemies." ⁴⁵But the disciples did not know what he meant. The meaning was hidden from them. They could not understand it, and they were afraid to ask.

Who is the greatest?

⁴⁶Jesus' disciples were arguing about which one of them was the greatest. ⁴⁷Jesus knew what they were thinking, and he had a child stand there beside him. ⁴⁸Then he said to his disciples, "When you welcome even a child because of me, you welcome me. And when you welcome me, you welcome the one who sent me. Whichever one of you is the most humble is the greatest."

For or against Jesus

⁴⁹John said, "Master, we saw a man using your name to force demons out of people. But we told him to stop, because he isn't one of us."

⁵⁰"Don't stop him!" Jesus said. "Anyone who isn't against you is for you."

A Samaritan village refuses to receive Jesus

⁵¹Not long before it was time for Jesus to be taken up to heaven, he made up his mind to go to Jerusalem. ⁵²He sent some messengers on ahead to a Samaritan village to get things ready for him. ⁵³But he was on his way to Jerusalem, so the people there refused to welcome him. ⁵⁴When the disciples James and John saw what was happening, they asked, "Lord, do you want us to call down fire from heaven to destroy these people?"*

⁵⁵But Jesus turned and corrected them for what they had said.* ⁵⁶Then they all went on to another village.

Three people who wanted to be followers

⁵⁷Along the way someone said to Jesus, "I'll go anywhere with you!"

⁵⁸Jesus said, "Foxes have dens, and birds have nests, but the Son of Man doesn't have a place to call his own."

⁵⁹Jesus told someone else to come with him. But the man said, "Lord, let me wait until I bury my father."*

⁶⁰Jesus answered, "Let the dead take care of the dead, while you go and tell about God's kingdom."

9.54 to destroy these people: Some manuscripts add "as Elijah did".
9.55 what they had said: Some manuscripts add, "and said, 'Don't you know what spirit you belong to? The Son of Man did not come to destroy people's lives, but to save them.' "

9.59 bury my father: The Jewish people taught that giving someone a proper burial was even more important than helping the poor.

⁶¹Then someone said to Jesus, "I want to go with you, Lord, but first let me go back and take care of things at home."

⁶²Jesus answered, "Anyone who starts ploughing and keeps looking back isn't worth a thing to God's kingdom!"

The work of the seventy-two followers

10 Later the Lord chose seventy-two* other followers and sent them out two by two to every town and village where he was about to go. ²He said to them:

A large crop is in the fields, but there are only a few workers. Ask the Lord in charge of the harvest to send out workers to bring it in. ³Now go, but remember, I am sending you like lambs into a pack of wolves. ⁴Don't take along a money bag or a travelling bag or sandals. And don't waste time greeting people on the road.*⁵As soon as you enter a home, say, "God bless this home with peace." ⁶If the people living there are peace-loving, your prayer for peace will bless them. But if they are not peace-loving, your prayer will return to you. ⁷Stay with the same family, eating and drinking whatever they give you, because workers are worth what they earn. Don't move around from house to house.

⁸If the people of a town welcome you, eat whatever they offer. ⁹Heal their sick and say, "God's kingdom will soon be here!"*

¹⁰But if the people of a town refuse to welcome you, go out into the street and say, ¹¹"We are shaking the dust from our feet* as a warning to you. And you can be sure that God's kingdom will soon be here!"* ¹²I tell you that on the day of judgment the people of Sodom will get off easier than the people of that town!

The unbelieving towns

Jesus continued:

¹³You people of Chorazin are in for trouble! You people of Bethsaida are also in for trouble! If the miracles that took place in your towns had happened in Tyre and Sidon, the people there would have turned to God long ago. They would have dressed in sackcloth and put ashes on their heads.* ¹⁴On the day of judgment the people of Tyre and Sidon will

10.1 seventy-two: Some manuscripts have "seventy". According to the book of Genesis, there were seventy nations on earth. But the ancient Greek translation of the Old Testament has "seventy-two" in place of "seventy". Jesus probably chose this number of followers to show that his message was for everyone in the world.
10.4 waste time greeting people on the road: In those days a polite greeting could take a long time.

10.9 will soon be here: Or "is already here".
10.11 shaking the dust from our feet: This was a way of showing rejection.
10.11 will soon be here: Or "is already here".
10.13 dressed in sackcloth…ashes on their heads: This was one way that people showed how sorry they were for their sins.

get off easier than you will. ¹⁵People of Capernaum, do you think you will be honoured in heaven? Well, you will go down to hell!

¹⁶My followers, whoever listens to you is listening to me. Anyone who says "No" to you is saying "No" to me. And anyone who says "No" to me is really saying "No" to the one who sent me.

The return of the seventy-two

¹⁷When the seventy-two* followers returned, they were excited and said, "Lord, even the demons obeyed when we spoke in your name!"

¹⁸Jesus told them:

I saw Satan fall from heaven like a flash of lightning. ¹⁹I have given you the power to trample on snakes and scorpions and to defeat the power of your enemy Satan. Nothing can harm you. ²⁰But don't be happy because evil spirits obey you. Be happy that your names are written in heaven!

Jesus thanks his Father

²¹At that same time, Jesus felt the joy that comes from the Holy Spirit,* and he said:

My Father, Lord of heaven and earth, I am grateful that you hid all this from wise and educated people and showed it to ordinary people. Yes, Father, that is what pleased you.

²²My Father has given me everything, and he is the only one who knows the Son. The only one who really knows the Father is the Son. But the Son wants to tell others about the Father, so that they can know him too.

²³Jesus then turned to his disciples and said to them in private, "You are really blessed to see what you see! ²⁴Many prophets and kings were eager to see what you see and to hear what you hear. But I tell you that they did not see or hear."

The good Samaritan

²⁵An expert in the Law of Moses stood up and asked Jesus a question to see what he would say. "Teacher," he asked, "what must I do to have eternal life?"

²⁶Jesus answered, "What is written in the Scriptures? How do you understand them?"

²⁷The man replied, "The Scriptures say, 'Love the Lord your God with all your heart, soul, strength, and mind.' They also say, 'Love your neighbours as much as you love yourself.' "

10.17 seventy-two: See the note at 10.1.   **10.21 the Holy Spirit:** Some manuscripts have "his spirit".

²⁸Jesus said, "You have given the right answer. If you do this, you will have eternal life."

²⁹But the man wanted to show that he knew what he was talking about. So he asked Jesus, "Who are my neighbours?"

³⁰Jesus replied:

As a man was going down from Jerusalem to Jericho, robbers attacked him and grabbed everything he had. They beat him up and ran off, leaving him half dead.

³¹A priest happened to be going down the same road. But when he saw the man, he walked by on the other side. ³²Later a temple helper* came to the same place. But when he saw the man who had been beaten up, he also went by on the other side.

³³A man from Samaria then came travelling along that road. When he saw the man, he felt sorry for him ³⁴and went over to him. He treated his wounds with olive oil and wine* and bandaged them. Then he put him on his own donkey and took him to an inn, where he took care of him. ³⁵The next morning he gave the innkeeper two silver coins and said, "Please take care of the man. If you spend more than this on him, I will pay you when I return."

³⁶Then Jesus asked, "Which one of these three people was a real neighbour to the man who was beaten up by robbers?"

³⁷The teacher answered, "The one who showed pity."

Jesus said, "Go and do the same!"

Martha and Mary

³⁸The Lord and his disciples were travelling along and came to a village. When they got there, a woman named Martha welcomed him into her home. ³⁹She had a sister named Mary, who sat down in front of the Lord and was listening to what he said. ⁴⁰Martha was worried about all that had to be done. Finally, she went to Jesus and said, "Lord, doesn't it bother you that my sister has left me to do all the work by myself? Tell her to come and help me!"

⁴¹The Lord answered, "Martha, Martha! You are worried and upset about so many things, ⁴²but only one thing is necessary. Mary has chosen what is best, and it will not be taken away from her."

Prayer

11 When Jesus had finished praying, one of his disciples said to him, "Lord, teach us to pray, just as John taught his followers to pray." ²So Jesus told them, "Pray in this way:

10.32 temple helper: A man from the tribe of Levi, whose job it was to work around the temple.

10.34 olive oil and wine: In New Testament times these were used as medicine. Sometimes olive oil is a symbol for healing by means of a miracle.

29:

'Father, help us to honour your name.
    Come and set up your kingdom.
³Give us each day the food we need.*
⁴Forgive our sins,
    as we forgive everyone who has done wrong to us.
And keep us from being tempted.' "

⁵Then Jesus went on to say:

Suppose one of you goes to a friend in the middle of the night and says, "Let me borrow three loaves of bread. ⁶A friend of mine has dropped in, and I don't have a thing for him to eat." ⁷And suppose your friend answers, "Don't bother me! The door is bolted, and my children and I are in bed. I cannot get up to give you something."

⁸He may not get up and give you the bread, just because you are his friend. But he will get up and give you as much as you need, simply because you are not ashamed to keep on asking.

⁹So I tell you to ask and you will receive, search and you will find, knock and the door will be opened for you. ¹⁰Everyone who asks will receive, everyone who searches will find, and the door will be opened for everyone who knocks. ¹¹Which one of you fathers would give your hungry child a snake if the child asked for a fish? ¹²Which one of you would give your child a scorpion if the child asked for an egg? ¹³As bad as you are, you still know how to give good gifts to your children. But your heavenly Father is even more ready to give the Holy Spirit to anyone who asks.

Jesus and the ruler of demons

¹⁴Jesus forced a demon out of a man who could not talk. And after the demon had gone out, the man started speaking, and the crowds were amazed. ¹⁵But some people said, "He forces out demons by the power of Beelzebul, the ruler of the demons!"

¹⁶Others wanted to put Jesus to the test. So they asked him to show them a sign from God. ¹⁷Jesus knew what they were thinking, and he said:

A kingdom where people fight each other will end up in ruin. And a family that fights will break up. ¹⁸If Satan fights against himself, how can his kingdom last? Yet you say that I force out demons by the power of Beelzebul. ¹⁹If I use his power to force out demons, whose power do your own followers use to force them out? They are the ones who will judge you. ²⁰But if I use God's power to force out demons, it proves that God's kingdom has already come to you.

11.3 the food we need: Or "food for today"
or "food for the coming day".

²¹When a strong man arms himself and guards his home, everything he owns is safe. ²²But if a stronger man comes and defeats him, he will carry off the weapons in which the strong man trusted. Then he will divide with others what he has taken. ²³If you are not on my side, you are against me. If you don't gather in the crop with me, you scatter it.

Return of an evil spirit

Jesus continued:

²⁴When an evil spirit leaves a person, it travels through the desert, looking for a place to rest. But when it doesn't find a place, it says, "I will go back to the home I left." ²⁵When it gets there and finds the place clean and tidy, ²⁶it goes off and finds seven other evil spirits even worse than itself. They all come and make their home there, and that person ends up in a worse state than before.

Being really blessed

²⁷While Jesus was still talking, a woman in the crowd spoke up, "The woman who gave birth to you and nursed you is blessed!"

²⁸Jesus replied, "That's true, but the people who are really blessed are the ones who hear and obey God's message!"*

A sign from God

²⁹As crowds were gathering around Jesus, he said:

You people of today are evil! You keep looking for a sign from God. But what happened to Jonah* is the only sign you will be given. ³⁰Just as Jonah was a sign to the people of Nineveh, the Son of Man will be a sign to the people of today. ³¹When the judgment comes, the Queen of the South* will stand there with you and condemn you. She travelled a long way to hear Solomon's wisdom, and yet here is something far greater than Solomon. ³²The people of Nineveh will also stand there with you and condemn you. They turned to God when Jonah preached, and yet here is something far greater than Jonah.

Light

Jesus continued:

³³No one lights a lamp and then hides it or puts it under a clay pot. A lamp is put on a lampstand, so that everyone who comes into the

11.28 "That's true, but the people who are really blessed...message": Or " 'That's not true, the people who are blessed . . . message.' "

11.29 what happened to Jonah: Jonah was in the stomach of a big fish for three days and nights.
11.31 Queen of the South: Sheba, probably a country in southern Arabia.

house can see the light. [34]Your eyes are the lamp for your body. When your eyes are good, you have all the light you need. But when your eyes are bad, everything is dark. [35]So be sure that your light isn't darkness. [36]If you have light, and nothing is dark, then light will be everywhere, as when a lamp shines brightly on you.

Jesus condemns the Pharisees and teachers of the Law of Moses

[37]When Jesus finished speaking, a Pharisee invited him home for a meal. Jesus went and sat down to eat.* [38]The Pharisee was surprised that he did not wash his hands* before eating. [39]So the Lord said to him:

You Pharisees clean the outside of cups and dishes, but on the inside you are greedy and evil. [40]You fools! Didn't God make both the outside and the inside?* [41]If you would only give what you have to the poor, everything you do would please God.

[42]You Pharisees are in for trouble! You give God a tenth of the spices from your gardens, such as mint and rue. But you cheat people, and you don't love God. You should be fair and kind to others and still give a tenth to God.

[43]You Pharisees are in for trouble! You love the front seats in the meeting places, and you like to be greeted with honour in the market. [44]But you are in for trouble! You are like unmarked graves* that people walk on without even knowing it.

[45]A teacher of the Law of Moses spoke up, "Teacher, you said cruel things about us."

[46]Jesus replied:

You teachers are also in for trouble! You load people down with heavy burdens, but you won't lift a finger to help them carry the loads. [47]Yes, you are really in for trouble. You build monuments to honour the prophets your own people murdered long ago. [48]You must think that was the right thing for your people to do, or else you would not have built monuments for the prophets they murdered.

[49]Because of your evil deeds, the Wisdom of God said, "I will send prophets and apostles to you. But you will murder some and ill-treat others." [50]You people living today will be punished for all the prophets

---

11.37 sat down to eat: See the note at 7.36.
11.38 did not wash his hands: The Jewish people had strict laws about washing their hands before eating, especially if they had been out in public.
11.40 Didn't God make both the outside and the inside?: Or "Doesn't the person who washes the outside always wash the inside too?"

11.44 unmarked graves: Tombs were whitewashed to keep anyone from accidentally touching them. A person who touched a dead body or a tomb was considered unclean and could not worship with other Jewish people.

who have been murdered since the beginning of the world. ⁵¹This includes every prophet from the time of Abel to the time of Zechariah,* who was murdered between the altar and the temple. You people will certainly be punished for all this.

⁵²You teachers of the Law of Moses are really in for trouble! You carry the keys to the door of knowledge about God. But you never go in, and you keep others from going in.

⁵³Jesus was about to leave, but the teachers and the Pharisees wanted to get even with him. They tried to make him say what he thought about other things, ⁵⁴so that they could catch him saying something wrong.

Warnings

12 As thousands of people crowded around Jesus and were stepping on each other, he told his disciples:

Be sure to guard against the dishonest teaching* of the Pharisees! It is their way of fooling people. ²Everything that is hidden will be found out, and every secret will be known. ³Whatever you say in the dark will be heard when it is day. Whatever you whisper in a closed room will be shouted from the housetops.

The one to fear

Jesus continued:

⁴My friends, don't be afraid of people. They can kill you, but after that, there is nothing else they can do. ⁵God is the one you must fear. Not only can he take your life, but he can throw you into hell. God is certainly the one you should fear!

⁶Five sparrows are sold for just two pennies, but God doesn't forget a single one of them. ⁷Even the hairs on your head are counted. So don't be afraid! You are worth much more than many sparrows.

Telling others about Christ

Jesus continued:

⁸If you tell others that you belong to me, the Son of Man will tell God's angels that you are my followers. ⁹But if you reject me, you will be rejected in front of them. ¹⁰If you speak against the Son of Man, you can be forgiven, but if you speak against the Holy Spirit, you cannot be forgiven.

11.51 from the time of Abel...Zechariah: Genesis is the first book in the Jewish Scriptures, and it tells that Abel was the first person to be murdered. The Second Book of Chronicles is the last book in the Jewish Scriptures, and the last murder that it tells about is that of Zechariah.

12.1 dishonest teaching: The Greek text has "yeast", which is used here of a teaching that is not true.

[11]"When you are brought to trial in the Jewish meeting places or before rulers or officials, don't worry about how you will defend yourselves or what you will say. [12]At that time the Holy Spirit will tell you what to say.

A rich fool

[13]A man in a crowd said to Jesus, "Teacher, tell my brother to give me my share of what our father left us when he died."

[14]Jesus answered, "Who gave me the right to settle arguments between you and your brother?"

[15]Then he said to the crowd, "Don't be greedy! Owning a lot of things won't make your life safe."

[16]So Jesus told them this story:

A rich man's farm produced a big crop, [17]and he said to himself, "What can I do? I don't have a place large enough to store everything." [18]Later, he said, "Now I know what I'll do. I'll tear down my barns and build bigger ones, where I can store all my grain and other goods. [19]Then I'll say to myself, 'You have stored up enough good things to last for years to come. Live it up! Eat, drink, and enjoy yourself.' "

[20]But God said to him, "You fool! Tonight you will die. Then who will get what you have stored up?"

[21]"This is what happens to people who store up everything for themselves, but are poor in the sight of God."

Worry

[22]Jesus said to his disciples:

I tell you not to worry about your life! Don't worry about having something to eat or wear. [23]Life is more than food or clothing. [24]Look at the crows! They don't plant or harvest, and they don't have storehouses or barns. But God takes care of them. You are much more important than any birds. [25]Can worry make you live longer?* [26]If you don't have power over small things, why worry about everything else?

[27]Look how the wild flowers grow! They don't work hard to make their clothes. But I tell you that Solomon with all his wealth* wasn't as well clothed as one of these flowers. [28]God gives such beauty to everything that grows in the fields, even though it is here today and thrown into a fire tomorrow. Won't he do even more for you? You have such little faith!

12.25 live longer: Or "grow taller".

12.27 Solomon with all his wealth: The Jewish people thought that Solomon was the richest person who had ever lived.

²⁹Don't keep worrying about having something to eat or drink. ³⁰Only people who don't know God are always worrying about such things. Your Father knows what you need. ³¹But put God's work first, and these things will be yours as well.

Treasures in heaven

Jesus continued:

³²My little group of disciples, don't be afraid! Your Father wants to give you the kingdom. ³³Sell what you have and give the money to the poor. Make yourselves money bags that never wear out. Make sure your treasure is safe in heaven, where thieves cannot steal it and moths cannot destroy it. ³⁴Your heart will always be where your treasure is.

Faithful and unfaithful servants

Jesus continued:

³⁵Be ready and keep your lamps burning ³⁶just like those servants who wait up for their master to return from a wedding feast. As soon as he comes and knocks, they open the door for him. ³⁷Servants are fortunate if their master finds them awake and ready when he comes! I promise you that he will get ready and have his servants sit down so he can serve them. ³⁸Those servants are really fortunate if their master finds them ready, even though he comes late at night or early in the morning. ³⁹You would not let a thief break into your home, if you knew when the thief was coming. ⁴⁰So always be ready! You don't know when the Son of Man will come.

⁴¹Peter asked Jesus, "Did you say this just for us or for everyone?" ⁴²The Lord answered:

Who are faithful and wise servants? Who are the ones the master will put in charge of giving the other servants their food supplies at the proper time? ⁴³Servants are fortunate if their master comes and finds them doing their job. ⁴⁴A servant who is always faithful will be put in charge of everything the master owns.

⁴⁵But suppose one of the servants thinks that the master won't return until late. Suppose that servant starts beating all the other servants and eats and drinks and gets drunk. ⁴⁶If that happens, the master will come on a day and at a time when the servant least expects him. That servant will then be punished and thrown out with the servants who cannot be trusted.

⁴⁷If servants are not ready or willing to do what their master wants them to do, they will be beaten hard. ⁴⁸But servants who don't know

what their master wants them to do will not be beaten so hard for doing wrong. If God has been generous with you, he will expect you to serve him well. But if he has been more than generous, he will expect you to serve him even better.

Not peace, but trouble

Jesus continued:

⁴⁹I came to set fire to the earth, and I wish it were already on fire! ⁵⁰I am going to be put to a hard test. And I will have to suffer a lot of pain until it is over. ⁵¹Do you think that I came to bring peace to earth? No indeed! I came to make people choose sides. ⁵²A family of five will be divided, with two of them against the other three. ⁵³Fathers and sons will turn against one another, and mothers and daughters will do the same. Mothers-in-law and daughters-in-law will also turn against each other.

Knowing what to do

⁵⁴Jesus said to all the people:

As soon as you see a cloud coming up in the west, you say, "It's going to rain," and it does. ⁵⁵When the south wind blows, you say, "It's going to get hot," and it does. ⁵⁶Are you trying to fool someone? You can predict the weather by looking at the earth and sky, but you don't really know what's going on right now. ⁵⁷Why don't you understand the right thing to do? ⁵⁸When someone accuses you of something, try to settle things before you are taken to court. If you don't, you will be dragged before the judge. Then the judge will hand you over to the jailer, and you will be locked up. ⁵⁹You won't get out until you have paid the last penny you owe.

Turn back to God

13 About this same time Jesus was told that Pilate had given orders for some people from Galilee to be killed while they were offering sacrifices. ²Jesus replied:

Do you think that these people were worse sinners than everyone else in Galilee just because of what happened to them? ³Not at all! But you can be sure that if you don't turn back to God, every one of you will also be killed. ⁴What about those eighteen people who died when the tower in Siloam fell on them? Do you think they were worse than everyone else in Jerusalem? ⁵Not at all! But you can be sure that if you don't turn back to God, every one of you will also die.

A story about a fig tree

⁶Jesus then told them this story:

A man had a fig tree growing in his vineyard. One day he went out to pick some figs, but he didn't find any. ⁷So he said to the gardener, "For three years I have come looking for figs on this tree, and I haven't found any yet. Chop it down! Why should it take up space?"

⁸The gardener answered, "Master, leave it for another year. I'll dig around it and put some manure on it to make it grow. ⁹Perhaps it will have figs on it next year. If it doesn't, you can have it cut down."

Healing a woman on the Sabbath

¹⁰One Sabbath, Jesus was teaching in a Jewish meeting place, ¹¹and a woman was there who had been crippled by an evil spirit for eighteen years. She was completely bent over and could not straighten up. ¹²When Jesus saw the woman, he called her over and said, "You are now well." ¹³He placed his hands on her, and at once she stood up straight and praised God.

¹⁴The man in charge of the meeting place was angry because Jesus had healed someone on the Sabbath. So he said to the people, "Each week has six days when we can work. Come and be healed on one of those days, but not on the Sabbath."

¹⁵The Lord replied, "Are you trying to fool someone? Won't any one of you untie your ox or donkey and lead it out to drink on a Sabbath? ¹⁶This woman belongs to the family of Abraham, but Satan has kept her bound for eighteen years. Isn't it right to set her free on the Sabbath?" ¹⁷Jesus' words made his enemies ashamed. But everyone else in the crowd was happy about the wonderful things he was doing.

A mustard seed and yeast

¹⁸Jesus said, "What is God's kingdom like? What can I compare it with? ¹⁹It is like what happens when someone plants a mustard seed in a garden. The seed grows as big as a tree, and birds nest in its branches."

²⁰Then Jesus said, "What can I compare God's kingdom with? ²¹It is like what happens when a woman mixes yeast into three batches of flour. Finally, all the dough rises."

The narrow door

²²As Jesus was on his way to Jerusalem, he taught the people in the towns and villages. ²³Someone asked him, "Lord, are only a few people going to be saved?"

Jesus answered:

²⁴Do all you can to go in by the narrow door! A lot of people will try to get in, but will not be able to. ²⁵Once the owner of the house gets up and locks the door, you will be left standing outside. You will knock on the door and say, "Sir, open the door for us!"

But the owner will answer, "I don't know a thing about you!"

²⁶Then you will start saying, "We dined with you, and you taught in our streets."

²⁷But he will say, "I really don't know who you are! Get away from me, you evil people!"

²⁸Then when you have been thrown outside, you will weep and grit your teeth because you will see Abraham and Isaac and all the prophets in God's kingdom. ²⁹People will come from all directions and sit down to feast in God's kingdom. ³⁰There the ones who are now least important will be the most important, and those who are now most important will be least important.

Jesus and Herod

³¹At that time some Pharisees came to Jesus and said, "You had better get away from here! Herod* wants to kill you."

³²Jesus said to them:

Go and tell that fox, "I am going to force out demons and heal people today and tomorrow, and three days later I'll have finished." ³³But I am going on my way today and tomorrow and the next day. After all, Jerusalem is the place where prophets are killed.

Jesus loves Jerusalem

Jesus continued:

³⁴Jerusalem, Jerusalem! Your people have killed the prophets and have stoned the messengers who were sent to you. I have often wanted to gather your people, as a hen gathers her chicks under her wings. But you wouldn't let me. ³⁵Now your temple will be deserted. You won't see me again until the time when you say,

"Blessed is the one who comes
in the name of the Lord."

Jesus heals a sick man

14 One Sabbath, Jesus was having dinner in the home of an important Pharisee, and everyone was carefully watching Jesus. ²All of a sudden a man with swollen legs stood up in front of him. ³Jesus turned and

13.31 Herod: Herod Antipas, the son of
Herod the Great.

asked the Pharisees and the teachers of the Law of Moses, "Is it right to heal on the Sabbath?" [4]But they did not say a word.

Jesus took hold of the man. Then he healed him and sent him away. [5]Afterwards, Jesus asked the people, "If your son or ox falls into a well, wouldn't you pull him out straight away, even on the Sabbath?" [6]There was nothing they could say.

How to be a guest

[7]Jesus saw how the guests had tried to take the best seats. So he told them:

[8]When you are invited to a wedding feast, don't sit in the best place. Someone more important may have been invited. [9]Then the one who invited you will come and say, "Give your place to this other guest!" You will be embarrassed and will have to sit in the worst place. [10]When you are invited to be a guest, go and sit in the worst place. Then the one who invited you may come and say, "My friend, take a better seat!" You will then be honoured in front of all the other guests. [11]If you put yourself above others, you will be put down. But if you humble yourself, you will be honoured.

[12]Then Jesus said to the man who had invited him:

When you give a dinner or a banquet, don't invite your friends and family and relatives and rich neighbours. If you do, they will invite you in return, and you will be paid back. [13]When you give a feast, invite the poor, the crippled, the lame, and the blind. [14]They cannot pay you back. But God will bless you and reward you when his people rise from death.

The great banquet

[15]After Jesus had finished speaking, one of the guests said, "The greatest blessing of all is to be at the banquet in God's kingdom!"

[16]Jesus told him:

A man once gave a great banquet and invited a lot of guests. [17]When the banquet was ready, he sent a servant to tell the guests, "Everything is ready! Please come."

[18]One guest after another started making excuses. The first one said, "I bought some land, and I've got to look it over. Please excuse me."

[19]Another guest said, "I bought five teams of oxen, and I need to try them out. Please excuse me."

[20]Still another guest said, "I have just got married, and I can't be there."

[21]The servant told his master what happened, and the master became so angry that he said, "Go as fast as you can to every street and alley in town! Bring in everyone who is poor or crippled or blind or lame."

²²When the servant returned, he said, "Master, I've done what you told me, and there is still plenty of room for more people."

²³His master then told him, "Go out along the back roads and lanes and make people come in, so that my house will be full. ²⁴Not one of the guests I first invited will get even a bite of my food!"

Being a disciple

²⁵Large crowds were walking along with Jesus, when he turned and said:

²⁶You cannot be my disciple, unless you love me more than you love your father and mother, your wife and children, and your brothers and sisters. You cannot come with me unless you love me more than you love your own life.

²⁷You cannot be my disciple unless you carry your own cross and come with me.

²⁸Suppose one of you wants to build a tower. What is the first thing you will do? Won't you sit down and figure out how much it will cost and if you have enough money to pay for it? ²⁹Otherwise, you will start building the tower, but not be able to finish. Then everyone who sees what is happening will laugh at you. ³⁰They will say, "You started building, but could not finish the job."

³¹What will a king do if he has only ten thousand soldiers to defend himself against a king who is about to attack him with twenty thousand soldiers? Before he goes out to battle, won't he first sit down and decide if he can win? ³²If he thinks he won't be able to defend himself, he will send messengers and ask for peace while the other king is still a long way off. ³³So then, you cannot be my disciple unless you give away everything you own.

Salt and light

Jesus continued:

³⁴Salt is good, but if it no longer tastes like salt, how can it be made to taste salty again? ³⁵It is no longer good for the soil or even for the manure pile. People simply throw it out. If you have ears, pay attention!

One sheep

15 Tax collectors* and sinners were all crowding around to listen to Jesus. ²So the Pharisees and the teachers of the Law of Moses started grumbling, "This man is friendly with sinners. He even eats with them."

15.1 Tax collectors: See the note at 3.12.

[3]Then Jesus told them this story:

[4]If any of you has a hundred sheep, and one of them gets lost, what will you do? Won't you leave the ninety-nine in the field and go and look for the lost sheep until you find it? [5]And when you find it, you will be so glad that you will put it on your shoulder [6]and carry it home. Then you will call in your friends and neighbours and say, "Let's celebrate! I've found my lost sheep."

[7]Jesus said, "In the same way there is more happiness in heaven because of one sinner who turns to God than over ninety-nine good people who don't need to."

One coin

[8]Jesus told the people another story:

What will a woman do if she has ten silver coins and loses one of them? Won't she light a lamp, sweep the floor, and look carefully until she finds it? [9]Then she will call in her friends and neighbours and say, "Let's celebrate! I've found the coin I lost."

[10]Jesus said, "In the same way God's angels are happy when even one person turns to him."

Two sons

[11]Jesus also told them another story:

Once a man had two sons. [12]The younger son said to his father, "Give me my share of the property." So the father divided his property between his two sons.

[13]Not long after that, the younger son packed up everything he owned and left for a foreign country, where he wasted all his money in wild living. [14]He had spent everything, when a bad famine spread through that whole land. Soon he had nothing to eat.

[15]He went to work for a man in that country, and the man sent him out to take care of his pigs.* [16]He would have been glad to eat what the pigs were eating,* but no one gave him a thing.

[17]Finally, he came to his senses and said, "My father's workers have plenty to eat, and here I am, starving to death! [18]I will go to my father and say to him, 'Father, I have sinned against God in heaven and against you. [19]I am no longer good enough to be called your son. Treat me like one of your workers.' "

15.15 pigs: The Jewish religion taught that pigs were not fit to eat or even to touch. A Jewish man would have felt terribly insulted if he had to feed pigs, much less eat with them.

15.16 what the pigs were eating: The Greek text has "(bean) pods", which came from a tree in Palestine. These were used to feed animals. Poor people sometimes ate them too.

²⁰The younger son got up and started back to his father. But when he was still a long way off, his father saw him and felt sorry for him. He ran to his son and hugged and kissed him.

²¹The son said, "Father, I have sinned against God in heaven and against you. I am no longer good enough to be called your son."

²²But his father said to the servants, "Hurry and bring the best clothes and put them on him. Give him a ring for his finger and sandals* for his feet. ²³Get the best calf and prepare it, so we can eat and celebrate. ²⁴This son of mine was dead, but has now come back to life. He was lost and has now been found." And they began to celebrate.

²⁵The elder son had been out in the field. But when he came near the house, he heard the music and dancing. ²⁶So he called one of the servants over and asked, "What's going on here?"

²⁷The servant answered, "Your brother has come home safe and sound, and your father ordered us to kill the best calf." ²⁸The elder brother got so angry that he would not even go into the house.

His father came out and begged him to go in. ²⁹But he said to his father, "For years I have worked for you like a slave and have always obeyed you. But you have never even given me a little goat, so that I could give a dinner for my friends. ³⁰This other son of yours wasted your money on prostitutes. And now that he has come home, you ordered the best calf to be killed for a feast."

³¹His father replied, "My son, you are always with me, and everything I have is yours. ³²But we should be glad and celebrate! Your brother was dead, but he is now alive. He was lost and has now been found."

A dishonest manager

16 Jesus said to his disciples:

A rich man once had a manager to take care of his business. But he was told that his manager was wasting money. ²So the rich man called him in and said, "What is this I hear about you? Tell me what you have done! You are no longer going to work for me."

³The manager said to himself, "What shall I do now that my master is going to fire me? I can't dig ditches, and I'm ashamed to beg. ⁴I know what I'll do, so that people will welcome me into their homes after I've lost my job."

⁵Then one by one he called in the people who were in debt to his master. He asked the first one, "How much do you owe my master?"

⁶"A hundred barrels of olive oil," the man answered.

15.22 ring…sandals: These show that the young man's father fully accepted him as his son. A ring was a sign of high position in the family. Sandals showed that he was a son instead of a slave, since slaves did not usually wear sandals.

So the manager said, "Take your bill and sit down and quickly write 'fifty'."

[7]The manager asked someone else who was in debt to his master, "How much do you owe?"

"A thousand sacks* of wheat," the man replied.

The manager said, "Take your bill and write 'eight hundred'."

[8]The master praised his dishonest manager for looking out for himself so well. That's how it is! The people of this world look out for themselves better than the people who belong to the light.

[9]My disciples, I tell you to use wicked wealth to make friends for yourselves. Then when it is gone, you will be welcomed into an eternal home. [10]Anyone who can be trusted in little matters can also be trusted in important matters. But anyone who is dishonest in little matters will be dishonest in important matters. [11]If you cannot be trusted with this wicked wealth, who will trust you with true wealth? [12]And if you cannot be trusted with what belongs to someone else, who will give you something that will be your own? [13]You cannot be the slave of two masters. You will like one more than the other or be more loyal to one than to the other. You cannot serve God and money.

Some sayings of Jesus

[14]The Pharisees really loved money. So when they heard what Jesus said, they made fun of him. [15]But Jesus told them:

You are always making yourselves look good, but God sees what is in your heart. The things that most people think are important are worthless as far as God is concerned.

[16]Until the time of John the Baptist, people had to obey the Law of Moses and the Books of the Prophets.* But since God's kingdom has been preached, everyone is trying hard to get in. [17]Heaven and earth will disappear before the smallest letter of the Law does.

[18]It is a terrible sin* for a man to divorce his wife and marry another woman. It is also a terrible sin for a man to marry a divorced woman.

Lazarus and the rich man

Jesus continued:

[19]There was once a rich man who wore expensive clothes and every day ate the best food. [20]But a poor beggar named Lazarus was brought to the gate of the rich man's house. [21]He was happy just to eat the scraps that fell from the rich man's table. His body was covered with sores, and

16.7 a thousand sacks: The Greek text has "a hundred measures", and each measure is about 300 kilogrammes.
16.16 the Law of Moses and the Books of the Prophets: The Jewish Scriptures, that is, the Old Testament.

16.18 a terrible sin: The Greek text uses a word that means the sin of being unfaithful in marriage.

dogs kept coming up to lick them. [22]The poor man died, and angels took him to the place of honour next to Abraham.*

The rich man also died and was buried. [23]He went to hell* and was suffering terribly. When he looked up and saw Abraham far off and Lazarus at his side, [24]he said to Abraham, "Have pity on me! Send Lazarus to dip his finger in water and touch my tongue. I'm suffering terribly in this fire."

[25]Abraham answered, "My friend, remember that while you lived, you had everything good, and Lazarus had everything bad. Now he is happy, and you are in pain. [26]And besides, there is a deep ditch between us, and no one from either side can cross over."

[27]But the rich man said, "Abraham, then please send Lazarus to my father's home. [28]Let him warn my five brothers, so they won't come to this horrible place."

[29]Abraham answered, "Your brothers can read what Moses and the prophets* wrote. They should pay attention to that."

[30]Then the rich man said, "No, that's not enough! If only someone from the dead would go to them, they would listen and turn to God."

[31]So Abraham said, "If they won't pay attention to Moses and the prophets, they won't listen even to someone who comes back from the dead."

Faith and service

17 Jesus said to his disciples:

There will always be something that causes people to sin. But anyone who causes them to sin is in for trouble. A person who causes even one of my little followers to sin [2]would be better off thrown into the ocean with a heavy stone tied around their neck. [3]So be careful what you do.

Correct any followers* of mine who sin, and forgive the ones who say they are sorry. [4]Even if one of them ill-treats you seven times in one day and says, "I am sorry," you should still forgive that person.

[5]The apostles said to the Lord, "Make our faith stronger!"
[6]Jesus replied:

If you had faith no bigger than a tiny mustard seed, you could tell this mulberry tree to pull itself up, roots and all, and to plant itself in the ocean. And it would!

16.22 the place of honour next to Abraham: The Jewish people thought that heaven would be a banquet that God would give for them. Abraham would be the most important person there, and the guest of honour would sit next to him.
16.23 hell: The Greek text has "hades", which the Jewish people often thought of as the place where the dead wait for the final judgment.

16.29 Moses and the prophets: The Jewish Scriptures, that is, the Old Testament.
17.3 followers: The Greek text has "brothers", which is often used in the New Testament for followers of Jesus.

⁷If your servant comes in from ploughing or from taking care of the sheep, would you say, "Welcome! Come on in and have something to eat"? ⁸No, you wouldn't say that. You would say, "Prepare me something to eat. Get ready to serve me, so I can have my meal. Then later on you can eat and drink." ⁹Servants don't deserve special thanks for doing what they are supposed to do. ¹⁰And that's how it should be with you. When you've done all you should, then say, "We are merely servants, and we have simply done our duty."

Ten men with leprosy

¹¹On his way to Jerusalem, Jesus went along the border between Samaria and Galilee. ¹²As he was going into a village, ten men with leprosy* came towards him. They stood at a distance ¹³and shouted, "Jesus, Master, have pity on us!"

¹⁴Jesus looked at them and said, "Go and show yourselves to the priests."*

On their way they were healed. ¹⁵When one of them discovered that he was healed, he came back, shouting praises to God. ¹⁶He bowed down at the feet of Jesus and thanked him. The man was from the country of Samaria.

¹⁷Jesus asked, "Weren't ten men healed? Where are the other nine? ¹⁸Why was this foreigner the only one who came back to thank God?" ¹⁹Then Jesus told the man, "You may get up and go. Your faith has made you well."

God's kingdom

²⁰Some Pharisees asked Jesus when God's kingdom would come. He answered, "God's kingdom isn't something you can see. ²¹There is no use saying, 'Look! Here it is' or 'Look! There it is.' God's kingdom is here with you."*

²²Jesus said to his disciples:

The time will come when you will long to see one of the days of the Son of Man, but you will not. ²³When people say to you, "Look there," or "Look here," don't go looking for him. ²⁴The day of the Son of Man will be like lightning flashing across the sky. ²⁵But first he must suffer terribly and be rejected by the people of today. ²⁶When the Son of Man comes, things will be just as they were when Noah lived. ²⁷People were eating, drinking, and getting married right up to the day when Noah went into the big boat. Then the flood came and drowned everyone on earth.

²⁸When Lot* lived, people were also eating and drinking. They were buying, selling, planting, and building. ²⁹But on the very day Lot left Sodom, fiery flames poured down from the sky and killed everyone. ³⁰The same will happen on the day when the Son of Man appears.

17.12 leprosy: See the note at 4.27.
17.14 show yourselves to the priests: See the note at 5.14.
17.21 here with you: Or "in your hearts".

17.27, 28 Noah…Lot: When God destroyed the earth by a flood, he saved Noah and his family. And when God destroyed the cities of Sodom and Gomorrah and the evil people who lived there, he rescued Lot and his family.

³¹At that time no one on a rooftop* should go down into the house to get anything. No one in a field should go back to the house for anything. ³²Remember what happened to Lot's wife.*

³³People who try to save their lives will lose them, and those who lose their lives will save them. ³⁴On that night two people will be sleeping in the same bed, but only one will be taken. The other will be left. ³⁵⁻³⁶Two women will be together grinding wheat, but only one will be taken. The other will be left.*

³⁷Then Jesus' disciples spoke up, "But where will this happen, Lord?"
Jesus said, "Where there is a corpse, there will always be buzzards."*

A widow and a judge

18

Jesus told his disciples a story about how they should keep on praying and never give up:

²In a town there was once a judge who didn't fear God or care about people. ³In that same town there was a widow who kept going to the judge and saying, "Make sure that I get fair treatment in court."

⁴For a while the judge refused to do anything. Finally, he said to himself, "Even though I don't fear God or care about people, ⁵I will help this widow because she keeps on bothering me. If I don't help her, she will wear me out."

⁶The Lord said:

Think about what that crooked judge said. ⁷Won't God protect his chosen ones who pray to him day and night? Won't he be concerned for them? ⁸He will hurry and help them. But when the Son of Man comes, will he find on this earth anyone with faith?

A Pharisee and a tax collector

⁹Jesus told a story to some people who thought they were better than others and who looked down on everyone else:

¹⁰Two men went into the temple to pray.* One was a Pharisee and the other a tax collector.* ¹¹The Pharisee stood over by himself and prayed,* "God, I thank you that I am not greedy, dishonest, and unfaithful in marriage like other people. And I am really glad that I am not like that tax collector over there. ¹²I go without eating* for two days a week, and I give you one tenth of all I earn."

17.31 rooftop: See the note at 5.19.
17.32 what happened to Lot's wife: She turned into a block of salt when she disobeyed God.
17.35, 36 will be left: Some manuscripts add, "Two men will be in the same field, but only one will be taken. The other will be left."
17.37 Where there is a corpse, there will always be buzzards: This saying may mean that when anything important happens, people soon know about it. Or the saying may mean that whenever something bad happens, curious people gather around

and stare. But the word translated "buzzard" also means "eagle" and may refer to the Roman army, which had an eagle as its symbol.
18.10 into the temple to pray: Jewish people usually prayed there early in the morning and late in the afternoon.
18.10 tax collector: See the note at 3.12.
18.11 stood over by himself and prayed: Some manuscripts have "stood up and prayed to himself".
18.12 without eating: See the note at 2.37.

46 :

¹³The tax collector stood off at a distance and did not think he was good enough even to look up towards heaven. He was so sorry for what he had done that he pounded his chest and prayed, "God, have pity on me! I am such a sinner."

¹⁴Then Jesus said, "When the two men went home, it was the tax collector and not the Pharisee who was pleasing to God. If you put yourself above others, you will be put down. But if you humble yourself, you will be honoured."

Jesus blesses little children

¹⁵Some people brought their little children for Jesus to bless. But when his disciples saw them doing this, they told the people to stop bothering him. ¹⁶So Jesus called the children over to him and said, "Let the children come to me! Don't try to stop them. People who are like these children belong to God's kingdom.* ¹⁷You will never get into God's kingdom unless you enter it like a child!"

A rich and important man

¹⁸An important man asked Jesus, "Good Teacher, what must I do to have eternal life?"

¹⁹Jesus said, "Why do you call me good? Only God is good. ²⁰You know the commandments: 'Be faithful in marriage. Do not murder. Do not steal. Do not tell lies about others. Respect your father and mother.' "

²¹He told Jesus, "I have obeyed all these commandments since I was a young man."

²²When Jesus heard this, he said, "There is one thing you still need to do. Go and sell everything you own! Give the money to the poor, and you will have riches in heaven. Then come and be my follower." ²³When the man heard this, he was sad, because he was very rich.

²⁴Jesus saw how sad the man was. So he said, "It's terribly hard for rich people to get into God's kingdom! ²⁵In fact, it's easier for a camel to go through the eye of a needle than for a rich person to get into God's kingdom."

²⁶When the crowd heard this, they asked, "How can anyone ever be saved?"

²⁷Jesus replied, "There are some things that people cannot do, but God can do anything."

²⁸Peter said, "Remember, we left everything to be your followers!"

²⁹Jesus answered, "You can be sure that anyone who gives up home or wife or brothers or family or children because of God's kingdom ³⁰will be given much more in this life. And in the future world they will have eternal life."

18.16 People who are like these children belong to God's kingdom: Or "God's kingdom belongs to people who are like these children."

Jesus again tells about his death

³¹Jesus took the twelve apostles aside and said:

We are now on our way to Jerusalem. Everything that the prophets wrote about the Son of Man will happen there. ³²He will be handed over to foreigners,* who will make fun of him, ill-treat him, and spit on him. ³³They will beat him and kill him, but three days later he will rise to life.

³⁴The apostles did not understand what Jesus was talking about. They could not understand, because the meaning of what he said was hidden from them.

Jesus heals a blind beggar

³⁵When Jesus was coming close to Jericho, a blind man sat begging beside the road. ³⁶The man heard the crowd walking by and asked what was happening. ³⁷Some people told him that Jesus from Nazareth was passing by. ³⁸So the blind man shouted, "Jesus, Son of David,* have pity on me!" ³⁹The people who were going along with Jesus told the man to be quiet. But he shouted even louder, "Son of David, have pity on me!"

⁴⁰Jesus stopped and told some people to bring the blind man over to him. When the blind man was getting near, Jesus asked, ⁴¹"What do you want me to do for you?"

"Lord, I want to see!" he answered.

⁴²Jesus replied, "Look and you will see! Your eyes are healed because of your faith." ⁴³Straight away the man could see, and he went with Jesus and started thanking God. When the crowds saw what happened, they praised God.

Zacchaeus

19 Jesus was going through Jericho, ²where a man named Zacchaeus lived. He was in charge of collecting taxes* and was very rich. ³⁻⁴Jesus was heading his way, and Zacchaeus wanted to see what he was like. But Zacchaeus was a short man and could not see over the crowd. So he ran ahead and climbed up into a sycamore tree.

⁵When Jesus got there, he looked up and said, "Zacchaeus, hurry down! I want to stay with you today." ⁶Zacchaeus hurried down and gladly welcomed Jesus.

⁷Everyone who saw this started grumbling, "This man Zacchaeus is a sinner! And Jesus is going home to eat with him."

⁸Later that day Zacchaeus stood up and said to the Lord, "I will give half of my property to the poor. And I will now pay back four times as much* to everyone I have ever cheated."

18.32 foreigners: The Romans, who ruled Judea at this time.
18.38 Son of David: The Jewish people expected the Messiah to be from the family of King David, and for this reason the Messiah was often called the "Son of David".

19.2 in charge of collecting taxes: See the note at 3.12.
19.8 pay back four times as much: Both Jewish and Roman law said that a person must pay back four times the amount that was taken.

⁹Jesus said to Zacchaeus, "Today you and your family have been saved,* because you are a true son of Abraham.* ¹⁰The Son of Man came to look for and to save people who are lost."

A story about ten servants

¹¹The crowd was still listening to Jesus as he was getting close to Jerusalem. Many of them thought that God's kingdom would soon appear, ¹²and Jesus told them this story:

A prince once went to a foreign country to be crowned king and then to return. ¹³But before leaving, he called in ten servants and gave each of them some money. He told them, "Use this to earn more money until I get back."

¹⁴But the people of his country hated him, and they sent messengers to the foreign country to say, "We don't want this man to be our king."

¹⁵After the prince had been made king, he returned and called in his servants. He asked them how much they had earned with the money they had been given.

¹⁶The first servant came and said, "Sir, with the money you gave me I have earned ten times as much."

¹⁷"That's fine, my good servant!" the king said. "Since you have shown that you can be trusted with a small amount, you will be given ten cities to rule."

¹⁸The second one came and said, "Sir, with the money you gave me, I have earned five times as much."

¹⁹The king said, "You will be given five cities."

²⁰Another servant came and said, "Sir, here is your money. I kept it safe in a handkerchief. ²¹You are a hard man, and I was afraid of you. You take what isn't yours, and you harvest crops you didn't plant."

²²"You worthless servant!" the king told him. "You have condemned yourself by what you have just said. You knew that I am a hard man, taking what isn't mine and harvesting what I've not planted. ²³Why didn't you put my money in the bank? On my return, I could have had the money together with interest."

²⁴Then he said to some other servants standing there, "Take the money away from him and give it to the servant who earned ten times as much."

²⁵But they said, "Sir, he already has ten times as much!"

²⁶The king replied, "Those who have something will be given more. But everything will be taken away from those who don't have anything. ²⁷Now bring me the enemies who didn't want me to be their king. Kill them while I watch!"

19.9 saved: Zacchaeus was Jewish, but it is only now that he is rescued from sin and placed under God's care.

19.9 son of Abraham: As used in this verse, the words mean that Zacchaeus is truly one of God's special people.

Jesus enters Jerusalem

²⁸When Jesus had finished saying all this, he went on towards Jerusalem. ²⁹As he was getting near Bethphage and Bethany on the Mount of Olives, he sent two of his disciples on ahead. ³⁰He told them, "Go into the next village, where you will find a young donkey that has never been ridden. Untie the donkey and bring it here. ³¹If anyone asks why you are doing that, just say, 'The Lord* needs it.' "

³²They went off and found everything just as Jesus had said. ³³While they were untying the donkey, its owners asked, "Why are you doing that?"

³⁴They answered, "The Lord* needs it."

³⁵Then they led the donkey to Jesus. They put some of their clothes on its back and helped Jesus get on. ³⁶And as he rode along, the people spread clothes on the road* in front of him. ³⁷When Jesus was setting off down the Mount of Olives, his large crowd of disciples were happy and praised God because of all the miracles they had seen. ³⁸They shouted,

"Blessed is the king who comes in the name of the Lord!
  Peace in heaven and glory to God."

³⁹Some Pharisees in the crowd said to Jesus, "Teacher, make your disciples stop shouting!"

⁴⁰But Jesus answered, "If they keep quiet, these stones will start shouting."

⁴¹When Jesus came closer and could see Jerusalem, he cried ⁴²and said:

Today your people don't know what will bring them peace! Now it is hidden from them. ⁴³Jerusalem, the time will come when your enemies will build walls around you to attack you. Armies will surround you and close in on you from every side. ⁴⁴They will level you to the ground and kill your people. Not one stone in your buildings will be left on top of another. This will happen because you did not see that God had come to save you.*

Jesus in the temple

⁴⁵When Jesus entered the temple, he started chasing out the people who were selling things. ⁴⁶He told them, "The Scriptures say, 'My house should be a place of worship.' But you have made it a place where robbers hide!"

⁴⁷Each day, Jesus kept on teaching in the temple. So the chief priests, the teachers of the Law of Moses, and some other important people tried to have him killed. ⁴⁸But they could not find a way to do it, because everyone else was eager to listen to him.

19.31 The Lord: Or "The master of the donkey".
19.34 The Lord: Or "The master of the donkey".
19.36 spread clothes on the road: This was one way that the Jewish people welcomed a famous person.

19.44 that God had come to save you: The Jewish people looked for the time when God would come and rescue them from their enemies. But when Jesus came, many of them refused to obey him.

A question about Jesus' authority

20 One day, Jesus was teaching in the temple and telling the good news. So the chief priests, the teachers, and the nation's leaders ²asked him, "What right do you have to do these things? Who gave you this authority?"

³Jesus replied, "I want to ask you a question. ⁴Who gave John the right to baptize? Was it God in heaven or merely some human being?"

⁵They talked this over and said to each other, "We can't say that God gave John this right. Jesus will ask us why we didn't believe John. ⁶And we can't say that it was merely some human who gave John the right to baptize. The crowd will stone us to death, because they think John was a prophet."

⁷So they told Jesus, "We don't know who gave John the right to baptize."

⁸Jesus replied, "Then I won't tell you who gave me the right to do what I do."

Tenants of a vineyard

⁹Jesus told the people this story:

A man once planted a vineyard and let it. Then he left the country for a long time. ¹⁰When it was time to harvest the crop, he sent a servant to ask the tenants for his share of the grapes. But they beat up the servant and sent him away without anything. ¹¹So the owner sent another servant. The tenants also beat him up. They insulted him terribly and sent him away without a thing. ¹²The owner sent a third servant. He was also beaten terribly and thrown out of the vineyard.

¹³The owner then said to himself, "What am I going to do? I know what. I'll send my son, the one I love so much. They will surely respect him!"

¹⁴When the tenants saw the owner's son, they said to one another, "Some day he will own the vineyard. Let's kill him! Then we can have it all for ourselves." ¹⁵So they threw him out of the vineyard and killed him.

Jesus asked, "What do you think the owner of the vineyard will do? ¹⁶I'll tell you what. He will come and kill those tenants and let someone else have his vineyard."

When the people heard this, they said, "This must never happen!"

¹⁷But Jesus looked straight at them and said, "Then what do the Scriptures mean when they say, 'The stone that the builders tossed aside is now the most important stone of all'? ¹⁸Anyone who stumbles over this stone will get hurt, and anyone it falls on will be smashed to pieces."

¹⁹The chief priests and the teachers of the Law of Moses knew that Jesus was talking about them when he was telling this story. They wanted to arrest him at once, but they were afraid of the people.

Paying taxes

[20]Jesus' enemies kept watching him closely, because they wanted to hand him over to the Roman governor. So they sent some men who pretended to be good. But they were really spies trying to catch Jesus saying something wrong. [21]The spies said to him, "Teacher, we know that you teach the truth about what God wants people to do. And you treat everyone with the same respect, no matter who they are. [22]Tell us, should we pay taxes to the Emperor or not?"

[23]Jesus knew that they were trying to trick him. So he told them, [24]"Show me a coin." Then he asked, "Whose picture and name are on it?"

"The Emperor's," they answered.

[25]Then he told them, "Give the Emperor what belongs to him and give God what belongs to God." [26]Jesus' enemies could not catch him saying anything wrong there in front of the people. They were amazed at his answer and kept quiet.

Life in the future world

[27]The Sadducees did not believe that people would rise to life after death. So some of them came to Jesus [28]and said:

Teacher, Moses wrote that if a married man dies and has no children, his brother should marry the widow. Their first son would then be thought of as the son of the dead brother.

[29]There were once seven brothers. The first one married, but died without having any children. [30]The second one married his brother's widow, and he also died without having any children. [31]The same thing happened to the third one. Finally, all seven brothers married that woman and died without having any children. [32]At last the woman died. [33]When God raises people from death, whose wife will this woman be? All seven brothers had married her.

[34]Jesus answered:

The people in this world get married. [35]But in the future world no one who is worthy to rise from death will either marry [36]or die. They will be like the angels and will be God's children, because they have been raised to life.

[37]In the story about the burning bush, Moses clearly shows that people will live again. He said, "The Lord is the God worshipped by Abraham, Isaac, and Jacob."* [38]So the Lord isn't the God of the dead, but of the living. This means that everyone is alive as far as God is concerned.

[39]Some of the teachers of the Law of Moses said, "Teacher, you have given a good answer!" [40]From then on, no one dared to ask Jesus any questions.

20.37 "The Lord is the God worshipped by Abraham, Isaac, and Jacob": Jesus argues that if God is worshipped by these three, they must be alive, because he is the God of the living.

About David's son

[41]Jesus asked, "Why do people say that the Messiah will be the son of King David?*[42]In the book of Psalms, David himself says,

'The Lord said to my Lord,
Sit at my right side*
　　[43]until I make your enemies into a footstool for you.'

[44]David spoke of the Messiah as his Lord, so how can the Messiah be his son?"

Jesus and the teachers of the Law of Moses

[45]While everyone was listening to Jesus, he said to his disciples:

[46]Guard against the teachers of the Law of Moses! They love to walk around in long robes, and they like to be greeted in the market. They want the front seats in the meeting places and the best seats at banquets. [47]But they cheat widows out of their homes and then pray long prayers just to show off. These teachers will be punished most of all.

A widow's offering

21 Jesus looked up and saw some rich people tossing their gifts into the offering box. [2]He also saw a poor widow putting in two pennies. [3]And he said, "I tell you that this poor woman has put in more than all the others. [4]Everyone else gave what they didn't need. But she is very poor and gave everything she had."

The temple will be destroyed

[5]Some people were talking about the beautiful stones used to build the temple and about the gifts that had been placed in it. Jesus said,[6]"Do you see these stones? The time is coming when not one of them will be left in place. They will all be knocked down."

Warning about trouble

[7]Some people asked, "Teacher, when will all this happen? How can we know when these things are about to take place?"

[8]Jesus replied:

Don't be fooled by those who will come and claim to be me. They will say, "I am Christ!" and "Now is the time!" But don't follow them. [9]When you hear about wars and riots, don't be afraid. These things will have to happen first, but that isn't the end.

[10]Nations will go to war against one another, and kingdoms will attack each other. [11]There will be great earthquakes, and in many places people

---

20.41 the son of King David: See the note at 18.38.

20.42 right side: The place of power and honour.

will starve to death and suffer terrible diseases. All sorts of frightening things will be seen in the sky.

¹²Before all this happens, you will be arrested and punished. You will be tried in your meeting places and put in jail. Because of me you will be placed on trial before kings and governors. ¹³But this will be your chance to tell about your faith.

¹⁴Don't worry about what you will say to defend yourselves. ¹⁵I will give you the wisdom to know what to say. None of your enemies will be able to oppose you or to say that you are wrong. ¹⁶You will be betrayed by your own parents, brothers, family, and friends. Some of you will even be killed. ¹⁷Because of me, you will be hated by everyone. ¹⁸But don't worry!* ¹⁹You will be saved by being faithful to me.

Jerusalem will be destroyed

Jesus continued:

²⁰When you see Jerusalem surrounded by soldiers, you will know that it will soon be destroyed. ²¹If you are living in Judea at that time, run to the mountains. If you are in the city, leave it. And if you are out in the country, don't go back into the city. ²²This time of punishment is what is written about in the Scriptures. ²³It will be an awful time for women who are expecting babies or nursing young children! Everywhere in the land people will suffer horribly and be punished. ²⁴Some of them will be killed by swords. Others will be carried off to foreign countries. Jerusalem will be overrun by foreign nations until their time comes to an end.

When the Son of Man appears

Jesus continued:

²⁵Strange things will happen to the sun, moon, and stars. The nations on earth will be afraid of the roaring sea and tides, and they won't know what to do. ²⁶People will be so frightened that they will faint because of what is happening to the world. Every power in the sky will be shaken.* ²⁷Then the Son of Man will be seen, coming in a cloud with great power and glory. ²⁸When all this starts happening, stand up straight and be brave. You will soon be set free.

A lesson from a fig tree

²⁹Then Jesus told them a story:

When you see a fig tree or any other tree ³⁰putting out leaves, you know that summer will soon come. ³¹So, when you see these things

21.18 But don't worry: The Greek text has "Not a hair of your head will be lost", which means, "There's no need to worry".

21.26 Every power in the sky will be shaken: In ancient times people thought that the stars were spiritual powers.

happening, you know that God's kingdom will soon be here. [32]You can be sure that some of the people of this generation will still be alive when all this takes place. [33]The sky and the earth won't last for ever, but my words will.

A warning

Jesus continued:

[34]Don't spend all your time thinking about eating or drinking or worrying about life. If you do, the final day will suddenly catch you [35]like a trap. That day will surprise everyone on earth. [36]Watch out and keep praying that you can escape all that is going to happen and that the Son of Man will be pleased with you.

[37]Jesus taught in the temple each day, and he spent each night on the Mount of Olives. [38]Everyone got up early and came to the temple to hear him teach.

A plot to kill Jesus

22 The Festival of Thin Bread, also called Passover, was near. [2]The chief priests and the teachers of the Law of Moses were looking for a way to get rid of Jesus, because they were afraid of what the people might do. [3]Then Satan entered the heart of Judas Iscariot,* who was one of the twelve apostles.

[4]Judas went to talk with the chief priests and the officers of the temple police about how he could help them arrest Jesus. [5]They were very pleased and offered to pay Judas some money. [6]He agreed and started looking for a good chance to betray Jesus when the crowds were not around.

Jesus eats with his disciples

[7]The day had come for the Festival of Thin Bread, and it was time to kill the Passover lambs. [8]So Jesus said to Peter and John, "Go and prepare the Passover meal for us to eat."

[9]But they asked, "Where do you want us to prepare it?"

[10]Jesus told them, "As you go into the city, you will meet a man carrying a jar of water.* Follow him into the house [11]and say to the owner, 'Our teacher wants to know where he can eat the Passover meal with his disciples.' [12]The owner will take you upstairs and show you a large room ready for you to use. Prepare the meal there."

[13]Peter and John left. They found everything just as Jesus had told them, and they prepared the Passover meal.

22.3 Iscariot: See the note at 6.16.

22.10 a man carrying a jar of water: A male slave carrying water would probably mean that the family was rich.

The Lord's supper

[14]When the time came for Jesus and the apostles to eat, [15]he said to them, "I have very much wanted to eat this Passover meal with you before I suffer. [16]I tell you that I will not eat another Passover meal until it is finally eaten in God's kingdom."

[17]Jesus took a cup of wine in his hands and gave thanks to God. Then he told the apostles, "Take this wine and share it with each other. [18]I tell you that I will not drink any more wine until God's kingdom comes."

[19]Jesus took some bread in his hands and gave thanks for it. He broke the bread and handed it to his apostles. Then he said, "This is my body, which is given for you. Eat this as a way of remembering me!"

[20]After the meal he took another cup of wine in his hands. Then he said, "This is my blood. It is poured out for you, and with it God makes his new agreement. [21]The one who will betray me is here at the table with me! [22]The Son of Man will die in the way that has been decided for him, but it will be terrible for the one who betrays him!"

[23]Then the apostles started arguing about who would ever do such a thing.

An argument about greatness

[24]The apostles got into an argument about which one of them was the greatest. [25]So Jesus told them:

Foreign kings order their people around, and powerful rulers call themselves everyone's friends.* [26]But don't be like them. The most important one of you should be like the least important, and your leader should be like a servant. [27]Who do people think is the greatest, a person who is served or one who serves? Isn't it the one who is served? But I have been with you as a servant.

[28]You have stayed with me in all my troubles. [29]So I will give you the right to rule as kings, just as my Father has given me the right to rule as a king. [30]You will eat and drink with me in my kingdom, and you will each sit on a throne to judge the twelve tribes of Israel.

Jesus' disciples will be tested

[31]Jesus said, "Simon, listen to me! Satan has demanded the right to test each one of you, as a farmer does when he separates wheat from the husks.* [32]But Simon, I have prayed that your faith will be strong. And when you have come back to me, help the others."

[33]Peter said, "Lord, I am ready to go with you to jail and even to die with you."

[34]Jesus replied, "Peter, I tell you that before a cock crows tomorrow morning, you will say three times that you don't know me."

22.25 everyone's friends: This translates a Greek word that rulers sometimes used as a title for themselves or for special friends.

22.31 separates wheat from the husks: See the note at 3.17.

Money bags, travelling bags, and swords

³⁵Jesus asked his disciples, "When I sent you out without a money bag or a travelling bag or sandals, did you need anything?"

"No!" they answered.

³⁶Jesus told them, "But now, if you have a money bag, take it with you. Also take a travelling bag, and if you don't have a sword,* sell some of your clothes and buy one. ³⁷Do this because the Scriptures say, 'He was considered a criminal.' This was written about me, and it will soon come true."

³⁸The disciples said, "Lord, here are two swords!"

"Enough of that!" Jesus replied.

Jesus prays

³⁹Jesus went out to the Mount of Olives, as he often did, and his disciples went with him. ⁴⁰When they got there, he told them, "Pray that you won't be tested."

⁴¹Jesus walked on a little way before he knelt down and prayed, ⁴²"Father, if you will, please don't make me suffer by having me drink from this cup.* But do what you want, and not what I want."

⁴³Then an angel from heaven came to help him. ⁴⁴Jesus was in great pain and prayed so sincerely that his sweat fell to the ground like drops of blood.*

⁴⁵Jesus got up from praying and went over to his disciples. They were asleep and worn out from being so sad. ⁴⁶He said to them, "Why are you asleep? Wake up and pray that you won't be tested."

Jesus is arrested

⁴⁷While Jesus was still speaking, a crowd came up. It was led by Judas, one of the twelve apostles. He went over to Jesus and greeted him with a kiss.*

⁴⁸Jesus asked Judas, "Are you betraying the Son of Man with a kiss?"

⁴⁹When Jesus' disciples saw what was about to happen, they asked, "Lord, should we attack them with a sword?" ⁵⁰One of the disciples even struck at the high priest's servant with his sword and cut off the servant's right ear.

⁵¹"Enough of that!" Jesus said. Then he touched the servant's ear and healed it.

⁵²Jesus spoke to the chief priests, the temple police, and the leaders who had come to arrest him. He said, "Why do you come out with swords and clubs and treat me like a criminal? ⁵³I was with you every day in the temple, and you didn't arrest me. But this is your time, and darkness* is in control."

22.36 money bag...travelling bag...sword:
These were things that someone would take on a dangerous journey. Jesus was telling his disciples to be ready for anything that might happen. They seem to have understood what he meant (see 22.49–51).
22.42 having me drink from this cup: In the Scriptures "to drink from a cup" sometimes means to suffer.

22.43, 44 Then an angel...like drops of blood: Verses 43, 44 are not in some manuscripts.
22.47 greeted him with a kiss: It was the custom for people to greet each other with a kiss on the cheek.
22.53 darkness: Darkness stands for the power of the devil.

Peter says he doesn't know Jesus

⁵⁴Jesus was arrested and led away to the house of the high priest, while Peter followed at a distance. ⁵⁵Some people built a fire in the middle of the courtyard and were sitting around it. Peter sat there with them, ⁵⁶and a servant girl saw him. Then after she had looked at him carefully, she said, "This man was with Jesus!"

⁵⁷Peter said, "Woman, I don't even know that man!"

⁵⁸A little later someone else saw Peter and said, "You are one of them!"

"No, I'm not!" Peter replied.

⁵⁹About an hour later another man insisted, "This man must have been with Jesus. They both come from Galilee."

⁶⁰Peter replied, "I don't know what you are talking about!" At once, while Peter was still speaking, a cock crowed.

⁶¹The Lord turned and looked at Peter. And Peter remembered that the Lord had said, "Before a cock crows tomorrow morning, you will say three times that you don't know me." ⁶²Then Peter went out and cried hard.

⁶³The men who were guarding Jesus made fun of him and beat him. ⁶⁴They put a blindfold on him and said, "Tell us who struck you!" ⁶⁵They kept on insulting Jesus in many other ways.

Jesus is questioned by the council

⁶⁶At daybreak the nation's leaders, the chief priests, and the teachers of the Law of Moses got together and brought Jesus before their council. ⁶⁷They said, "Tell us! Are you the Messiah?"

Jesus replied, "If I said so, you wouldn't believe me. ⁶⁸And if I asked you a question, you wouldn't answer. ⁶⁹But from now on, the Son of Man will be seated at the right side of God All-Powerful."

⁷⁰Then they asked, "Are you the Son of God?"*

Jesus answered, "You say I am!"*

⁷¹They replied, "Why do we need more witnesses? He said it himself!"

Pilate questions Jesus

23 Everyone in the council got up and led Jesus off to Pilate. ²They started accusing him and said, "We caught this man trying to get our people to riot and to stop paying taxes to the Emperor. He also claims that he is the Messiah, our king."

³Pilate asked Jesus, "Are you the king of the Jews?"

"Those are your words," Jesus answered.

⁴Pilate told the chief priests and the crowd, "I don't find him guilty of anything."

22.70 Son of God: This was one of the titles used for the kings of Israel.

22.70 You say I am: Or "That's what you say."

[5]But they all kept on saying, "He has been teaching and causing trouble all over Judea. He started in Galilee and has now come all the way here."

Jesus is brought before Herod

[6]When Pilate heard this, he asked, "Is this man from Galilee?" [7]After Pilate learnt that Jesus came from the region ruled by Herod,* he sent him to Herod, who was in Jerusalem at that time.

[8]For a long time Herod had wanted to see Jesus and was very happy because he finally had this chance. He had heard many things about Jesus and hoped to see him perform a miracle.

[9]Herod asked him a lot of questions, but Jesus did not answer. [10]Then the chief priests and the teachers of the Law of Moses stood up and accused him of all kinds of bad things.

[11]Herod and his soldiers made fun of Jesus and insulted him. They put a fine robe on him and sent him back to Pilate. [12]That same day Herod and Pilate became friends, even though they had been enemies before this.

The death sentence

[13]Pilate called together the chief priests, the leaders, and the people. [14]He told them, "You brought Jesus to me and said he was a troublemaker. But I have questioned him here in front of you, and I have not found him guilty of anything that you say he has done. [15]Herod didn't find him guilty either and sent him back. This man doesn't deserve to be put to death! [16-17]I will just have him beaten with a whip and set free."*

[18]But the whole crowd shouted, "Kill Jesus! Give us Barabbas!" [19]Now Barabbas was in jail because he had started a riot in the city and had murdered someone.

[20]Pilate wanted to set Jesus free, so he spoke again to the crowds. [21]But they kept shouting, "Nail him to a cross! Nail him to a cross!"

[22]Pilate spoke to them a third time, "But what crime has he done? I have not found him guilty of anything for which he should be put to death. I will have him beaten with a whip and set free."

[23]The people kept on shouting as loud as they could for Jesus to be put to death. [24]Finally, Pilate gave in. [25]He freed the man who was in jail for rioting and murder, because he was the one the crowd wanted to be set free. Then Pilate handed Jesus over for them to do what they wanted with him.

23.7 Herod: Herod Antipas, the son of Herod the Great.

23.16, 17 set free: Some manuscripts add, "Pilate said this, because at every Passover he was supposed to set one prisoner free for the Jewish people."

Jesus is nailed to a cross

²⁶As Jesus was being led away, some soldiers grabbed hold of a man from Cyrene named Simon. He was coming in from the fields, but they put the cross on him and made him carry it behind Jesus.

²⁷A large crowd was following Jesus, and in the crowd a lot of women were crying and weeping for him. ²⁸Jesus turned to the women and said:

Women of Jerusalem, don't cry for me! Cry for yourselves and for your children. ²⁹Some day people will say, "Women who never had children are really fortunate!" ³⁰At that time everyone will say to the mountains, "Fall on us!" They will say to the hills, "Hide us!" ³¹If this can happen when the wood is green, what do you think will happen when it is dry?*

³²Two criminals were led out to be put to death with Jesus. ³³When the soldiers came to the place called "The Skull",* they nailed Jesus to a cross. They also nailed the two criminals to crosses, one on each side of Jesus.

³⁴⁻³⁵Jesus said, "Father, forgive these people! They don't know what they're doing."*

While the crowd stood there watching Jesus, the soldiers gambled for his clothes. The leaders insulted him by saying, "He saved others. Now he should save himself, if he really is God's chosen Messiah!"

³⁶The soldiers made fun of Jesus and brought him some wine. ³⁷They said, "If you are the king of the Jews, save yourself!"

³⁸Above him was a sign that said, "This is the King of the Jews."

³⁹One of the criminals hanging there also insulted Jesus by saying, "Aren't you the Messiah? Save yourself and save us!"

⁴⁰But the other criminal told the first one off, "Don't you fear God? Aren't you getting the same punishment as this man? ⁴¹We got what was coming to us, but he didn't do anything wrong." ⁴²Then he said to Jesus, "Remember me when you come into power!"

⁴³Jesus replied, "I promise that today you will be with me in paradise."*

The death of Jesus

⁴⁴Around midday the sky turned dark and stayed that way until the middle of the afternoon. ⁴⁵The sun stopped shining, and the curtain in the temple*

23.31 If this can happen when the wood is green, what do you think will happen when it is dry?: This saying probably means, "If this can happen to an innocent person, what do you think will happen to one who is guilty?"

23.33 "The Skull": The place was probably given this name because it was near a large rock in the shape of a human skull.

23.34, 35 Jesus said, "Father, forgive these people! They don't know what they're doing.": These words are not in some manuscripts.

23.43 paradise: In the Greek translation of the Old Testament, this word is used for the Garden of Eden. In New Testament times it was sometimes used for the place where God's people are happy and at rest, as they wait for the final judgment.

23.45 curtain in the temple: There were two curtains in the temple. One was at the entrance, and the other separated the holy place from the most holy place that the Jewish people thought of as God's home on earth. The second curtain is probably the one which is meant.

split down the middle. ⁴⁶Jesus shouted, "Father, I put myself in your hands!" Then he died.

⁴⁷When the Roman officer saw what had happened, he praised God and said, "Jesus must really have been a good man!"

⁴⁸A crowd had gathered to see the terrible sight. Then after they had seen it, they felt brokenhearted and went home. ⁴⁹All Jesus' close friends and the women who had come with him from Galilee stood at a distance and watched.

Jesus is buried

⁵⁰⁻⁵¹There was a man named Joseph, who was from Arimathea in Judea. Joseph was a good and honest man, and he was eager for God's kingdom to come. He was also a member of the Jewish council, but he did not agree with what they had decided.

⁵²Joseph went to Pilate and asked for Jesus' body. ⁵³He took the body down from the cross and wrapped it in fine cloth. Then he put it in a tomb that had been cut out of solid rock and had never been used. ⁵⁴It was Friday, and the Sabbath was about to begin.*

⁵⁵The women who had come with Jesus from Galilee followed Joseph and watched how Jesus' body was placed in the tomb. ⁵⁶Then they went to prepare some sweet-smelling spices for his burial. But on the Sabbath they rested, as the Law of Moses commands.

Jesus is alive

24 Very early on Sunday morning the women went to the tomb, carrying the spices that they had prepared. ²When they found the stone rolled away from the entrance, ³they went in. But they did not find the body of the Lord* Jesus, ⁴and they did not know what to think.

Suddenly two men in shining white clothes stood beside them. ⁵The women were afraid and bowed to the ground. But the men said, "Why are you looking in the place of the dead for someone who is alive? ⁶Jesus isn't here! He has been raised from death. Remember that while he was still in Galilee, he told you, ⁷'The Son of Man will be handed over to sinners who will nail him to a cross. But three days later he will rise to life.' " ⁸Then they remembered what Jesus had said.

⁹⁻¹⁰Mary Magdalene, Joanna, Mary the mother of James, and some other women were the ones who had gone to the tomb. When they returned, they told the eleven apostles and the others what had happened. ¹¹The apostles thought it was all nonsense, and they would not believe.

23.54 the Sabbath was about to begin: The Sabbath begins at sunset on Friday.

24.3 the Lord: These words are not in some manuscripts.

61:

[12]But Peter ran to the tomb. And when he stooped down and looked in, he saw only the burial clothes. Then he returned, wondering what had happened.*

Jesus appears to two disciples

[13]That same day two of Jesus' disciples were going to the village of Emmaus, which was about eleven kilometres from Jerusalem. [14]As they were talking and thinking about what had happened, [15]Jesus came near and started walking along beside them. [16]But they did not know who he was.

[17]Jesus asked them, "What were you talking about as you walked along?"

The two of them stood there looking sad and gloomy. [18]Then the one named Cleopas asked Jesus, "Are you the only person from Jerusalem who didn't know what was happening there these last few days?"

[19]"What do you mean?" Jesus asked.

They answered:

Those things that happened to Jesus from Nazareth. By what he did and said he showed that he was a powerful prophet, who pleased God and all the people. [20]Then the chief priests and our leaders had him arrested and sentenced to die on a cross. [21]We had hoped that he would be the one to set Israel free! But it has already been three days since all this happened.

[22]Some women in our group surprised us. They had gone to the tomb early in the morning, [23]but did not find the body of Jesus. They came back, saying that they had seen a vision of angels who told them that he is alive. [24]Some men from our group went to the tomb and found it just as the women had said. But they didn't see Jesus either.

[25]Then Jesus asked the two disciples, "Why can't you understand? How can you be so slow to believe all that the prophets said? [26]Didn't you know that the Messiah would have to suffer before he was given his glory?" [27]Jesus then explained everything written about himself in the Scriptures, beginning with the Law of Moses and the Books of the Prophets.*

[28]When the two of them came near the village where they were going, Jesus seemed to be going farther. [29]They begged him, "Stay with us! It's already late, and the sun is going down." So Jesus went into the house to stay with them.

24.12 what had happened: Verse 12 is not in some manuscripts.

24.27 the Law of Moses and the Books of the Prophets: The Jewish Scriptures, that is, the Old Testament.

³⁰After Jesus sat down to eat, he took some bread. He blessed it and broke it. Then he gave it to them. ³¹At once they knew who he was, but he disappeared. ³²They said to each other, "When he talked with us along the road and explained the Scriptures to us, didn't it warm our hearts?" ³³So they got up at once and returned to Jerusalem.

The two disciples found the eleven apostles and the others gathered together. ³⁴And they learnt from the group that the Lord was really alive and had appeared to Peter. ³⁵Then the disciples from Emmaus told what happened on the road and how they knew he was the Lord when he broke the bread.

What Jesus' followers must do

³⁶While Jesus' disciples were talking about what had happened, Jesus appeared and greeted them. ³⁷They were frightened and terrified because they thought they were seeing a ghost.

³⁸But Jesus said, "Why are you so frightened? Why do you doubt? ³⁹Look at my hands and my feet and see who I am! Touch me and find out for yourselves. Ghosts don't have flesh and bones as you see I have."

⁴⁰After Jesus said this, he showed them his hands and his feet. ⁴¹The disciples were so glad and amazed that they could not believe it. Jesus then asked them, "Do you have something to eat?" ⁴²They gave him a piece of baked fish. ⁴³He took it and ate it as they watched.

⁴⁴Jesus said to them, "While I was still with you, I told you that everything written about me in the Law of Moses, the Books of the Prophets, and in the Psalms* had to happen."

⁴⁵Then he helped them understand the Scriptures. ⁴⁶He told them:

The Scriptures say that the Messiah must suffer, then three days later he will rise from death. ⁴⁷They also say that all people of every nation must be told in my name to turn to God, in order to be forgiven. So beginning in Jerusalem, ⁴⁸you must tell everything that has happened. ⁴⁹I will send you the one my Father has promised,* but you must stay in the city until you are given power from heaven.

Jesus returns to heaven

⁵⁰Jesus led his disciples out to Bethany, where he raised his hands and blessed them. ⁵¹As he was doing this, he left and was taken up to heaven.*

24.44 Psalms: The Jewish Scriptures were made up of three parts: (1) the Law of Moses, (2) the Books of the Prophets, (3) and the Writings, which included the Psalms. Sometimes the Scriptures were just called the Law or the Law (of Moses) and the Books of the Prophets.

24.49 the one my Father has promised: Jesus means the Holy Spirit.
24.51 and was taken up to heaven: These words are not in some manuscripts.

⁵²After his disciples had worshipped him,* they returned to Jerusalem and were very happy. ⁵³They spent their time in the temple, praising God.

**24.52 After his disciples had worshipped
him:** These words are not in some manuscripts.

Luke's gospel

General terms

Angel   A divine messenger appearing in human form but obviously supernatural. The one who spoke to Mary and to Zechariah was named Gabriel.

Cross   A Roman form of drawn-out execution, designed to cause maximum suffering as a deterrent to criminals. To cause his death, Jesus would have been nailed to a cross through his wrists and feet.

Devil   The chief spiritual being in opposition to God's intentions for the created world and humankind.

Disciple   A pupil or follower. Luke's name for the followers of John the Baptist and Jesus.

Heaven   The state where God dwells along with his angels, and where all his people go after this life. It is the state where the will of God is perfectly expressed.

Hell   In contrast to heaven, expressed in images of dreadful torment. The after-world of unbelievers separated from God.

Holy Spirit   Third person of the Godhead, at work in the world today.

Kingdom of God   The Kingdom or rule of God is a central theme of Jesus' teaching. In his life and work God's reign begins to take shape, though its full manifestation lies in the future.

Law   Usually refers to the first five books of the Old Testament and sometimes to the Ten Commandments, given by God to Moses.

1400AD

Printing press invented   **Christopher Columbus**

Prophet	Someone called by God to proclaim his message. The writings and teachings of the prophets make up one of the three divisions of the Jewish Scriptures (the Old Testament).
Samaritans	A mixed-race people living in Samaria between Judea and Galilee, and despised by Jews.
Sinners	Those considered at the time to be beyond the pale of God's concern, and therefore unable to be saved. These included non-Jews and breakers of the religious laws.
Tax collectors	The Roman occupiers employed Jewish tax collectors who were considered to be traitors by the people.

Terms used for Jesus

Christ	The Greek term for the Messiah meaning "anointed by God" to perform a special work, especially rescue his people and to reign over them.
Son of God	A title which came to be used of Jesus both as Messiah and as his being one with his Father, i.e. fully divine as well as fully human.
Son of Man	Jesus probably took this title for himself from the Old Testament book of Daniel, where it is used of the coming Messiah.

1500ᴀᴅ

William Tyndale is burnt

1600ᴀᴅ

Pilgrim Fathers reach New England

Religious details

Passover A major Jewish festival celebrating the release of Israelite slaves from Egypt under the leadership of Moses. A key element was the sacrificial death of lambs to turn away the plague of death that afflicted Egypt. Christ's death took place at Passover time.

Pharisees A rigid religious group among the Jews. They added many detailed regulations to the laws in the Old Testament.

Priests Probably as many as 7,000 priests were actively involved in temple worship in Jerusalem at the time of Jesus. Their main task was to offer animal sacrifices.

Sabbath The seventh and holy day of the Jewish week, beginning at sunset on the Friday; a strict day of rest.

Sadducees An aristocratic and predominantly lay religious group who accepted only the first five books of the Old Testament, and were sceptical of supernatural elements of belief such as the resurrection of the body.

Temple The centre of Jewish worship located in Jerusalem and destroyed by the Romans in AD 70.

Pudding Lane

Great Fire of London   *American Independence*   **1700**AD

People in Luke's story

12:

Annas — Appointed high priest in AD 6 and deposed in AD 15, yet still referred to as high priest (see Luke 3.2).

Barabbas — Arrested for political terrorism, and released by Pilate as a substitute for Jesus.

Caesar — Roman Emperor. Caesar Augustus, great-nephew of Julius Caesar, ruled from 30 BC to AD 14. He was succeeded by his step-son and son-in-law, Tiberius Caesar, emperor throughout Jesus' adult life.

Caiaphas — High priest AD 18—37, working in close co-operation with his father-in-law, Annas.

Herod — In his Gospel Luke mentions two people called Herod. (1) Luke 1.5 refers to Herod the Great, ruler of Judea from 37 to 4 BC. (2) All other references in Luke's Gospel are to Herod Antipas, ruler of Galilee from 4 BC to AD 39.

Jesus — The name means saviour or rescuer. He is the subject of Luke's Gospel, born 4—6 BC and died probably AD 33. Luke records his fully human nature, and triumph over death as Son of God.

John the disciple — Son of Zebedee, brother of James, fisherman and one of Jesus' first and closest followers.

Judas Iscariot — The disciple who betrayed Jesus. He probably came from Kerioth, hence, Iscariot. He was responsible for the finances of the band of disciples.

Levi — Also called Matthew, a tax collector who abandoned his trade to follow Jesus as a disciple.

1800AD

Karl Marx is born

Social reforms during Industrial Revolution

Peter A fisherman with his brother Andrew, Peter became a natural leader among Jesus' first followers.

Pilate Appointed as Roman prefect of Judea in AD 26, he had a stormy relationship with the Jewish authorities.

Theophilus A name meaning "friend of God". Probably an actual Greek person of high rank, or possibly a general term for the Christian reader.

People from the Old Testament

Abel The Bible's first murder victim, second son of Adam and Eve, the parents of the human race.

Abraham The first of the three great ancestors of the people of Israel — best known for his complete trust in God.

David Israel's greatest king (c. 1000 BC), an ancestor of Jesus Christ. Under David the nation's territory became greater than ever before.

Elijah One the greatest Old Testament prophets (ninth century BC).

Elisha Elijah's successor, who healed the non-Jewish Naaman of a severe skin disease.

Isaac Son of Abraham, one of the patriarchs of the Jewish people.

Isaiah Eighth-century BC prophet whose prophecies are recorded in the Old Testament, and much quoted by Luke.

Great Exhibition

1914AD

World War I

Jacob	Grandson of Abraham and son of Isaac, one of the patriarchs of the Jewish people.
Jonah	The Old Testament prophet ordered by God to preach to non-Jews in Nineveh. Their subsequent repentance is noted by Jesus (p.31, Luke 11.29—32).
Lot	Nephew of the patriarch Abraham who escaped the city of Sodom just before its destruction.
Moses	Jewish leader (c. 1250 BC) who led the Israelites out of slavery in Egypt and to whom God gave the Ten Commandments. See Law.
Naaman	A Syrian general of the ninth century BC who was healed of a disfiguring skin disease by the Jewish prophet, Elisha.
Queen of the South	Another name for the Queen of Sheba who visited King Solomon, son of David.

Places in Luke's story

Bethlehem	A town 8 km south-west of Jerusalem, in the Judean hills, the birthplace of Jesus.
Capernaum	An important fishing town on the north-west shore of the region. Levi and Peter's family lived here.
Galilee	A region in northern Israel which included the large lake of Galilee and Jesus' home town, Nazareth. Much of Jesus' teaching and healing took place here.

1939AD → → → **1950/60**AD

World War II   **TV increasingly available**

Jericho	One of the world's most ancient towns, located 250 m below sea level about 8 km north of the Dead Sea.
Jerusalem	Capital city and spiritual centre of the ancient Jewish kingdom. Jerusalem stands 770 m up in the Judean hills. In Jesus' day the temple was located there. It was destroyed by the Romans in AD 70.
Judea	A region of Palestine, the others being Samaria and Galilee.
Lake of Galilee or Gennesaret	A large lake (21 km long and 11 km broad) in the region of Galilee, kept fresh by the River Jordan running through it. Surrounded by hills, it is liable to atmospheric down-draughts and sudden storms.
Mount of Olives	A hill, 830 m in height, overlooking Jerusalem and its temple area from the east. It was reached by crossing the Kidron Valley.
Nazareth	A town in which Jesus grew up and worked as a carpenter.
Samaria	The capital of the Northern Kingdom of Israel before the Exile. The inhabitants of the area (Samaritans) had much in common with the Jews, but there was conflict between the two groups at the time of Jesus.
Sodom	A place of evil in the Old Testament, the ancient city is now probably covered by the Dead Sea.

1969AD

Moon landing

1989AD

Berlin wall comes down

Reading Luke's story can bring out all kinds of feelings. Take time to reflect. To discover what a difference being a follower of Jesus Christ can make to life, talk to someone who is already a Christian.

If you want to pray, tell God how you are feeling. **Know that God will welcome you.** He has given you many gifts, so be thankful. If you are sad, anxious or lonely, remember how Jesus was no stranger to suffering. God has been there, and he is with you now.

It's not always easy to find the right words to pray, and many Christians have used the words of others to express themselves. There is Jesus' own prayer on page 30 (Luke 11.2—4). Or, here is a prayer by a great Christian called Augustine:

Lord Jesus, I am seeking: I am hesitant and uncertain, but will you, my Lord and King, watch over each step I take, and guide me into your truth?

2000AD